FIRE

ON THE EARTH

Eyewitness Reports from the Azusa Street Revival

Commissioned for the
AZUSA STREET CENTENNIAL

DR. EDDIE HYATT, EDITOR

CREATION
HOUSE
A STRANG COMPANY

FIRE ON THE EARTH
Edited by Eddie Hyatt
Published by Creation House
A Strang Company
600 Rinehart Road
Lake Mary, Florida 32746
www.creationhouse.com

The publisher has retained the original spelling used in *The Apostolic Faith* articles, which are in the public domain.

Photos courtesy of Dixon Pentecostal Research Center

Cover design by Terry Clifton

Library of Congress Control Number: 2005939118
International Standard Book Number: 1-59185-924-7

First Edition

06 07 08 09 10 — 9 8 7 6 5 4 3 2 1
Printed in the United States of America

DEDICATION

THIS BOOK IS respectfully dedicated to the memory of Robert E. Fisher and to the passion of his life to bring spiritual renewal and unity to the body of Christ. It was through his vision that the Azusa Street Centennial was conceived and developed.

Robert E. Fisher was the grandson of Elmer K. Fisher, pastor of the First Baptist Church of Glendale, California, and one of the early participants and leaders in the Azusa Street revival of 1906. It was Robert Fisher's passion that the Holy Spirit, which empowered this revival a century ago, igniting Pentecostal fires around the world, would impact and anoint spiritual leaders anew for the task of the next century in a worldwide gathering. He laid the foundation for such a gathering, the Azusa Street Centennial, in Los Angeles, California, April 25–29, 2006. The theme he promoted for the event was, "Together Again, 2006."

Robert Fisher's life was a model of commitment and dedication in...

- His love for his beloved wife, Mary, whom he adored; his children, Robert, Cameron and Lorri, of whom he was very proud; and their spouses and his grandchildren who brought him great joy.

- His visionary leadership in numerous offices and positions of honor and influence.

- The utilization of God-given talents as husband,

father, grandfather, ordained bishop, minister, pastor, educator, communicator, counselor, mentor, author, and administrator.

The passion of a man's life does not die. It lives long after more temporal things fade. It is with honor and great respect that we dedicate this historical compilation of the original Azusa Street papers to our brother and friend, Dr. Robert E. Fisher.

—BOARD OF DIRECTORS
CENTER FOR SPIRITUAL RENEWAL
CLEVELAND, TENNESSEE

Dr. Robert E. Fisher, 1931–2005

CONTENTS

The Asberry home at 214 North Bonnie Brae Street where the revival began

312 Azusa Street in later years

PREFACE

THE CENTER FOR Spiritual Renewal is excited to present this compilation of the original papers published during the Azusa Street Revival. *Fire on the Earth* is not meant to be an exhaustive volume of those papers, which were called *The Apostolic Faith*. Rather, we have commissioned Dr. Eddie Hyatt to compile these in an easily readable book form, while maintaining the integrity of the original documents. Dr. Hyatt has sought to reduce repetition and capture the highlights of each edition of *The Apostolic Faith*. We appreciate his excellent work with this material and believe that the format of this book will be a blessing to thousands of believers around the world. We have included a basic index to help you connect with events of particular interest. If an historical fact from the original papers is missing, please be assured that no malice to anyone has been intended.

As you read through these wonderful, historical accounts, our prayer is that God will once again ignite your heart with the fire that burned brightly at Azusa Street and that God would send forth a fresh fire on the earth in our generation.

—CENTER FOR SPIRITUAL RENEWAL
BOARD OF DIRECTORS

Members of the First AME Church, which worshiped at
312 Azusa Street until 1904

312 Azusa Street at the height of the revival (the man in front
of the building is most likely William Seymour)

Introduction

THIS VOLUME CONTAINS selected excerpts from the original publication of the Azusa Street Revival that occurred in Los Angeles, California, from 1906–1909. Between September 1906 and May 1908, William J. Seymour and the leadership of the revival published thirteen issues of this paper that they called *The Apostolic Faith*. The name expressed their belief that, through this revival, the apostolic faith of the New Testament was being restored to the churches. The popularity of the paper increased dramatically and soon reached a distribution of forty thousand. Through its distribution, news of the revival was spread abroad and 312 Azusa Street became a legendary address in the annals of American revivalism.

Anyone reading these papers cannot help but sense the fervency and intensity of these saints who believed that the outpouring of the Spirit they were experiencing was God's final call before the end of the age. By reading this volume, perhaps the present generation will catch some of the fire that burned in the bosom of those early Pentecostal saints. Like the saints at Azusa Street, perhaps this generation too will ignite revival fire that will spread throughout the earth.

How the Fire of God Fell at Azusa

On April 9, 1906, the fire of God fell on a small group of hungry believers at a home on Bonnie Brae Street in downtown Los Angeles, California. Within a week the meetings moved to an old, dilapidated building located at 312 Azusa Street. For the

1

next three years services continued around the clock as thousands came from across the nation and around the world to experience the fire of a new Pentecostal outpouring of the Holy Spirit. This revival, led by a son of former slaves, ignited a movement that now numbers 600 million worldwide and is growing at the rate of 9 million per year.[1] In 1999 the prestigious Religion Newswriters Association included the Azusa Street Revival in their list of the "top ten" religious stories of the past millennia, alongside the Protestant Reformation and the publication of the Gutenberg Bible.[2] Their reason for including the Azusa Street Revival on this illustrious list was that it had given birth to the Pentecostal-Charismatic movement, "now Christianity's fastest growing branch."[3]

The Azusa Street Revival was birthed in a milieu of prayer and the belief that God would restore to the church the power of New Testament Christianity just before the return of Christ to the earth. The nineteenth century had witnessed the erosion of many people's faith through the emergence of Darwinian evolution and higher biblical criticism. Many Christians believed that only a restoration of the Pentecostal power of the New Testament would stem the tide of skepticism and unbelief. As the twentieth century dawned many were, therefore, praying for a revival of biblical proportions that would result in world evangelization and usher in the Second Coming of Christ.

WILLIAM J. SEYMOUR

Perhaps nowhere was the desire for revival more intense than in Los Angeles, California. Dissatisfied with traditional forms of Christianity and alarmed by the skepticism that seemed to permeate so many of the churches, scores of individuals and small groups were giving themselves to intense times of prayer. It was into this intense spiritual atmosphere that William J. Seymour arrived from Houston in February of 1906 to pastor a small storefront mission.

Seymour was born in 1870 in Centerville, Louisiana, into the home of former slaves, Simon and Phyllis Seymour. He attended the local black Baptist church with his parents and even as a child had a pronounced inclination toward the things of God. In 1892 at the age of twenty-two, he left the segregated south and lived for a time in Indianapolis and then in Cincinnati. In 1903 Seymour returned to Houston where he attended a black holiness church pastored by a woman named Lucy Farrow.

During the summer of 1905 Charles F. Parham came to Houston and conducted a citywide crusade in Bryan Hall. Parham preached a baptism in the Holy Spirit evidenced by speaking in tongues that he described as "a gift of power on the sanctified life." Parham found many receptive souls in Houston including Lucy Farrow who heartily embraced his message of a Spirit baptism evidenced by speaking in tongues. She developed a friendship with the Parhams, and when they returned to their home in Baxter Springs they invited her to go with them and act as a governess to their children. Farrow accepted the invitation and turned the pastorate of her congregation over to Seymour. While staying in the Parham home in Baxter Springs, she experienced her own Spirit baptism and spoke in tongues.

In the fall of 1905 Farrow, who was the niece of the famous abolitionist Frederick Douglas, returned with the Parhams to Houston and another crusade was held at Bryan Hall. After the crusade Parham began plans for a Bible school which would open on January 1, 1906. Farrow told Seymour of the school and encouraged him to attend. Having a deep hunger for more of God, he immediately applied for admission. His application created somewhat of a problem because of southern Jim Crow laws and customs that mandated the segregation of blacks and whites. Parham skirted these issues by allowing Seymour to sit in an adjoining room where he could listen to the classes through an open door. Here he drank in the teaching of a baptism in the Holy Spirit evidenced by speaking in tongues.

THE INVITATION TO LOS ANGELES

It was while he was attending classes and continuing to pastor his congregation in Houston that Seymour received the invitation to Los Angeles. Although Seymour did not receive the baptism in the Holy Spirit while in Houston, he was convinced of its veracity and had decided to preach it without compromise. In his first service at the mission in Los Angeles he, therefore, broached the subject of an experience called the baptism in the Holy Spirit evidenced by speaking in tongues. His audience, however, equated the baptism in the Holy Spirit with their experience of sanctification and did not believe tongues to be necessary. When Seymour returned for the evening service he found the door padlocked. The elders had decided that he was preaching false doctrine and chose to lock him out.

SEYMOUR AND INTENSE PRAYER

Some of the members had compassion on Seymour, and he was invited to stay in the homes of Edward Lee and then Richard Asberry. Having an intense hunger for the life and power of the Holy Spirit, Seymour gave himself to almost constant prayer. He later said:

> Before I met Parham, such a hunger to have more of God was in my heart that I prayed for five hours a day for two and a half years. I got to Los Angeles, and there the hunger was not less but more. I prayed, "God, what can I do?" The Spirit said, "Pray more." "But Lord, I am praying five hours a day now." I increased my hours of prayer to seven, and prayed on for a year and a half more. I prayed to God to give what Parham preached, the real Holy Ghost and fire with tongues with love and power of God like the apostles had.[4]

Noticing that their new guest was spending much of his time in prayer, the Asberrys decided to open their home at 214 Bonnie Brae Street to evening prayer meetings. In the course of these gatherings, Seymour shared with the group about Lucy Farrow who was the first to tell him about the baptism in the Holy Spirit and who had already received the experience. They were so anxious to meet her that they took up an offering for her train fare and invited her to come.

A few days later Edward Lee returned home after work to find Farrow who had just arrived from Houston. He was so hungry for the baptism in the Holy Spirit that after a brief introduction he implored, "Sister, if you will lay your hands on me I believe I will get my baptism right now." She replied, "I cannot do it unless the Lord says so." Later, while eating dinner, Farrow rose from her seat, walked over to Lee and said, "The Lord tells me to lay my hands on you for the Holy Ghost." She then laid her hands on Lee who immediately fell out of his chair and, while lying on the floor, began speaking in tongues.[5]

REVIVAL BREAKS FORTH

Later that same day the Lees and Farrow went to the Asberry home for the evening prayer meeting. As Edward Lee walked through the door, he lifted his hands and began speaking in tongues. Suddenly the power of God fell, and virtually everyone present began speaking in tongues. One of those present was Jennie Moore who later became Seymour's wife. She not only spoke in tongues but went to the piano and played and sang in tongues even though she had never had a lesson.[6] An eyewitness to these events said:

> They shouted three days and three nights. It was the Easter season. The people came from everywhere. By the next morning there was no way of getting near the house. As

the people came in they would fall under God's power; and the whole city was stirred. They shouted there until the foundation of the house gave way, but no one was hurt. During those three days there were many people who received their baptism. The sick were healed and sinners were saved just as they came in.[7]

Realizing that the Asberry home was too small to contain the crowds, Seymour and others began looking for larger facilities for their prayer meeting. They finally located an older dilapidated building at 312 Azusa Street in downtown Los Angeles. This 40' x 60' two-story structure had formerly been a Methodist Episcopal Church, but more recently had been used as a stable and warehouse. They removed the debris and installed rough plank benches and a makeshift pulpit made from wooden shoeboxes. On April 14, 1906, they held their first meeting in the new facilities, and revival fires blazed even more brightly.

THE PRIORITY OF PRAYER AT AZUSA

Although the prayer meeting was soon organized into a church that they called the Apostolic Faith Mission, prayer continued to be the foremost activity. One participant said, "The whole place was steeped in prayer."[8] Seymour, the recognized leader, spent much of his time behind the pulpit with his head inside the top shoebox praying. An unpretentious man, he recognized his own need for the continual guidance and strength of the Holy Spirit. A contemporary, John G. Lake, described him as a man of great spiritual power. He says:

> God had put such a hunger into that man's heart that when the fire of God came it glorified him. I do not believe any other man in modern times had a more wonderful deluge of God in his life than God gave to that dear fellow, and the glory and power of a real Pentecost swept the world.

That black man preached to my congregation of ten thousand people when the glory and power of God was upon his spirit, and men shook and trembled and cried to God. God was in him.[9]

HOLY SPIRIT LEADERSHIP

The services at Azusa were spontaneous. There were no pre-announced events, no special choirs, singers, or well-known evangelists. With no platform, everyone was on the same level, and anyone was free to share a testimony or word of exhortation. Although the building was never empty of people at prayer, the services usually began spontaneously around mid-morning and continued until three or four the following morning. One participant gave this description of the revival:

> The services ran almost continuously. Seeking souls could be found under the power almost any hour, day or night. In that old building God took strong men and women to pieces, and put them together again for his glory. Those were Holy Ghost meetings, led of the Lord. God's presence became more and more wonderful. The shekinah glory rested there. In fact some claim to have seen the glory by night over the building. I do not doubt it. I have stopped more than once within two blocks of the place and prayed for strength before I dared go on. The presence of the Lord was so real.[10]

Although dramatic spiritual manifestations captured the attention of the general public, walking in God's love was the primary emphasis at Azusa Street. Frank Bartleman, a journalist and participant in the revival, described it as a return to the "first love" of the early church.

> Divine love was wonderfully manifest in the meetings. They would not even allow an unkind word said against

any of their opposers, or the churches. The message was the love of God. It was a sort of "first love" of the early church returned. The "baptism" as we received it in the beginning did not allow us to think, speak, or hear evil of any man. We knew the moment we had grieved the Spirit by an unkind thought or word. We seemed to live in a sea of pure divine love.[11]

THE CROWDS COME TO AZUSA

As services continued at the Azusa Street Mission, the news spread by word of mouth and religious periodicals that God was doing a unique work there. *The Los Angeles Times* gave local coverage that, although it was not positive, caught the attention of the local populace. Bartleman wrote articles about the revival and sent them to Holiness publications throughout the country. Seymour began the paper preserved in this volume known as *The Apostolic Faith*.

News of the revival raised interest everywhere, and soon the faithful and the curious were journeying from far and near to experience the event. They came from across the United States and Canada. Missionaries on foreign soil heard of the revival and came. Visitors claimed that they could feel a supernatural atmosphere within several blocks of the mission.[12] Multitudes received the Pentecostal experience and went forth with new zeal, fresh vision, and a new message of Spirit-empowerment for world evangelism.

Many Christian leaders were impacted by the revival, and this resulted in several small holiness denominations being swept into Pentecostalism. In addition, many new Pentecostal churches began to arise as the Azusa pilgrims spread the fire of a new Pentecost everywhere they went. One of those whose life was transformed at the Azusa Street Mission was Ernest S. Williams who later served as general superintendent of the

Assemblies of God (1929–1949). He first visited the revival in 1907 and was astounded by what he encountered.

> I wish I could describe what I saw. Prayer and worship were everywhere. The altar area was filled with seekers; some were kneeling; others were prone on the floor; some were speaking in tongues. Everyone was doing something; all were seemingly lost in God. I simply stood and looked, for I had never seen anything like it.[13]

Shortly thereafter, Williams received his own personal Pentecost and spoke in tongues. Almost sixty years later, he revealed that that initial encounter with the Holy Spirit had not remained a unique experience.

> Soon it will be 59 years since I was filled with the Holy Spirit. I still have my seasons of refreshing from the presence of the Lord, speaking in other tongues and at times shaking under the influence of the Holy Spirit.[14]

Racial and Gender Equality in the Revival

In the beginning, the Azusa Mission was completely interracial at a time when segregation was an accepted social pattern in America. Bartleman said, "The color line was washed away in the blood."[16] Also, at a time when women were not allowed to vote, they enjoyed equal participation in leadership and ministry at Azusa. The original Azusa board of directors was made up of seven women and five men. Five of the women were white and two were black. Of the three men, two were white and one, Pastor Seymour, was black.

THE SIGNIFICANCE OF
THE AZUSA STREET REVIVAL

The revival continued unabated for about three years. During this time, Pentecostalism became a worldwide phenomenon. Ultimately, however, strife dampened the flames of revival, and as it smoldered, many whites left to begin their own churches and missions. By 1914 the Azusa Street Mission had become a small local black congregation. Seymour continued as the senior pastor until his death on September 28, 1922, in Los Angeles. His wife then served as pastor until her death in 1936. Eventually, the mission was sold and torn down to make room for a parking lot.

Seymour and Azusa Street, however, had carved for themselves a prominent place in the annals of church history. God used them as a catalyst to help spread the fire of Pentecostal revival around the world. Dr. Harvey Cox of the Harvard Divinity School says that the movement that has emerged out of that old, dilapidated building at 312 Azusa Street "is reshaping religion in the 21st century."[17]

One

PENTECOST HAS COME, SEPTEMBER 1906

THE APOSTOLIC FAITH

"Earnestly contend for the faith which was once delivered unto the saints." —Jude 3

Vol. 1, No. 1, Los Angeles, Cal., September, 1906, Subscription Free

LOS ANGELES BEING VISITED BY A REVIVAL OF BIBLE SALVATION AND PENTECOST AS RECORDED IN THE BOOK OF ACTS

The power of God now has this city agitated as never before. Pentecost has surely come and with it the Bible evidences are following, many being converted and sanctified and filled with the Holy Ghost, speaking in tongues as they did on the day of Pentecost. The scenes that are daily enacted in the building on Azusa Street and at Missions and churches in other parts of the city are beyond description, and the real revival is only started, as God has been working with His children mostly, getting them through to Pentecost, and laying the foundation for a mighty wave of salvation among the unconverted.

The meetings are held in an old Methodist church that had been converted in part into a tenement house, leaving a large, unplastered, barn-like room on the ground floor. Here about a dozen congregated each day, holding meetings on Bonnie Brae in the evening. The writer attended a few of these meetings and being so different from anything he had seen and not hearing any speaking in tongues, he branded the teaching as third-blessing heresy and thought that settled it. It is needless to say the writer was compelled to do a great deal of apologizing and humbling himself to get right with God.

In a short time God began to manifest His power and soon the building could not contain the people. Proud, well-dressed preachers come in to "investigate." Soon their high looks are replaced with wonder, then conviction comes, and very often you will find them in a short time wallowing on the dirty floor, asking God to forgive them and make them as little children.

It would be impossible to state how many have been converted, sanctified and filled with the Holy Ghost. They have been and are daily going out to all points of the compass to spread this wonderful gospel.

BRO. SEYMOUR'S CALL

Bro. W. J. Seymour has the following to say in regard to his call to this city:

"It was the divine call that brought me from Houston, Texas, to Los Angeles. The Lord put it in the heart of one of the saints in Los Angeles to write to me that she felt the Lord would have me come over here and do a work, and I came to take charge of a mission on Santa Fe Street, and one night they locked the door against me, and afterwards got Bro. Roberts, the president of the Holiness Association, to come down and settle the doctrine of the Baptism with the Holy Ghost, that it was simply sanctification. He came down and a good many holiness preachers with him, and they stated that sanctification was the baptism with the Holy Ghost. But yet they did not have the evidence of the second chapter of Acts, for when the disciples were all filled with the Holy Ghost, they spoke in tongues as the Spirit gave utterance. After the president heard me speak of what the true baptism of the Holy Ghost was, he said he wanted it too, and told me when I had received to let him know. So I received it and let him know. The beginning of the Pentecost started in a cottage prayer meeting at 214 Bonnie Brae."

LETTER FROM BRO. PARHAM

Bro. Chas. Parham, who is God's leader in the Apostolic Faith Movement, writes from Tonganoxie, Kansas, that he expects (D. V.) to be in Los Angeles Sept. 15. Hearing that Pentecost had come to Los Angeles, he writes, "I rejoice in God over you all, my children, though I have never seen you; but since you know the Holy Spirit's power, we are baptised by one Spirit into one body. Keep together in unity until I come, then in a grand meeting let all prepare for the outside fields I desire, unless God directs to the contrary, to meet and see all who have the full Gospel when I come."

THE OLD-TIME PENTECOST

This work began about five years ago last January, when a company of people under the leadership of Chas. Parham, who were studying God's word, tarried for Pentecost in Topeka, Kan. After searching through the country everywhere, they had been unable to find any Christians that had the true Pentecostal power. So they laid aside all commentaries and notes and waited on the Lord, studying His word, and what they did not understand they got down before the bench and asked to have wrought out in their hearts by the Holy Ghost. They had a prayer tower from which

prayers were ascending night and day to God. After three months, a sister who had been teaching sanctification for the baptism with the Holy Ghost, one who had a sweet, loving experience and all the carnality taken out of her heart, felt the Lord lead her to have hands laid on her to receive the Pentecost. So when they prayed, the Holy Ghost came in great power, and she commenced speaking an unknown tongue. This made all the Bible school hungry, and three nights afterward, twelve students received the Holy Ghost, and prophesied, and cloven tongues could be seen upon their heads. They then had an experience that measured up with the second chapter of Acts, and could understand the first chapter of Ephesians.

Now after five years something like 13,000 people have received this gospel. It is spreading everywhere, until churches who do not believe backslide and lose the experience they have. Those who are older in this movement are stronger, and greater signs and wonders are following them.

The meetings in Los Angeles started in a cottage meeting, and the Pentecost fell there three nights. The people had nothing to do but wait on the Lord and praise Him, and they commenced speaking in tongues, as they did at Pentecost, and the Spirit sang songs through them.

The meeting was then transferred to Azusa Street, and since then multitudes have been coming. The meetings begin about ten o'clock in the morning and can hardly stop before ten or twelve at night, and sometimes two or three in the morning, because so many are seeking, and some are slain under the power of God. People are seeking three times a day at the altar and row after row of seats have to be emptied and filled with seekers. We cannot tell how many people have been saved, and sanctified, and baptised with the Holy Ghost, and healed of all manner of sicknesses. Many are speaking in new tongues, and some are on their way to the foreign fields, with the gift of the language. We are going on to get more of the power of God.

Many have laid aside their glasses and had their eye sight perfectly restored. The deaf have had their hearing restored.

A man was healed of of twenty years standing. Many have been healed of heart trouble and lung trouble.

Many are saying that God has given the message that He is going to shake Los Angeles with an earthquake. First, there will be a revival to give all an opportunity to be saved. The revival is now in progress.

The Lord has given the gift of writing in unknown languages, also the gift of play on instruments.

A little girl who walked with crutches and had tuberculosis of the bones, as the doctors declared, was healed and dropped her crutches and began to skip about the yard.

All over this city, God has been setting homes on fire and coming down and melting and saving and sanctifying and baptizing with the Holy Ghost.

Many churches have been praying for Pentecost, and Pentecost has come. The question is now, will they accept it? God has answered in a way they did not look for. He came in a humble way as of old, born in a manger.

The secular papers have been stirred and published reports against the movement, but it has only resulted in drawing hungry souls who understand that the devil would not fight a thing unless God was in it. So they have come and found it was indeed the power of God.

Jesus was too large for the synagogues. He preached outside because there was not room for him inside. This Pentecostal movement is too large to be confined in any denomination or sect. It works outside, drawing all together in one bond of love, one church, one body of Christ.

A Mohammedan, a Soudanese by birth, a man who is an interpreter and speaks sixteen languages, came into the meetings at Azusa Street and the Lord gave him messages which none but himself could understand. He identified, interpreted and wrote in a number of the languages.

A brother who had been a spiritualist medium and who was so possessed with demons that he had no rest, and was on the point of committing suicide, was instantly delivered of demon power. He then sought God for the pardon of his sins and sanctification, and is now filled with a different spirit.

A little girl about twelve years of age was sanctified in a Sunday afternoon children's meeting, and in the evening meeting she was baptized with the Holy Ghost. When she was filled those standing near remarked, "Who can doubt such a clear case of God's power?"

In about an hour and a half, a young man was converted, sanctified, and baptized with the Holy Ghost, and spoke with tongues. He was also healed from consumption, so that when he visited the doctor he pronounced his lungs sound. He has received many tongues, also the gift of prophecy, and writing in a number of foreign languages, and has a call to a foreign field.

Many are the prophesies spoken in unknown tongues and many the visions that God is giving concerning His soon coming. The heathen must first receive the gospel. One prophecy given in an unknown tongue was interpreted, "The time is short, and I am going to send out a large number in the Spirit of God

to preach the full gospel in the power of the Spirit."

About 150 people in Los Angeles, more than on the day of Pentecost, have received the gift of the Holy Ghost and the Bible evidence, the gift of tongues, and many have been saved and sanctified, nobody knows how many. People are seeking at the altar three times a day and it is hard to close at night on account of seekers and those who are under the power of God.

When Pentecostal lines are struck, Pentecostal giving commences. Hundreds of dollars have been laid down for the sending of missionaries and thousands will be laid down. No collections are taken for rent, no begging for money. No man's silver or gold is coveted. The silver and the gold are His own to carry on His own work. He can also publish His own papers without asking for money or subscription price.

In the meetings, it is noticeable that while some in the rear are opposing and arguing, others are at the altar falling down under the power of God and feasting on the good things of God. The two spirits are always manifest, but no opposition can kill, no power in earth or hell can stop God's work, while He has consecrated instruments through which to work.

Many have received the gift of singing as well as speaking in the inspiration of the Spirit. The Lord is giving new voices, he translates old songs into new tongues, he gives the music that is being sung by the angels and has a heavenly choir all singing the same heavenly song in harmony. It is beautiful music, no instruments are needed in the meetings.

A Nazarene brother who received the baptism with the Holy Ghost in his own home in family worship, in trying to tell about it, said, "It was such a baptism of love. Such abounding love! Such compassion seemed to almost kill me with its sweetness! People do not know what they are doing when they stand against it. The devil never gave me a sweet thing, he was always trying to get me to censuring people. This baptism fills us with divine love."

The gift of languages is given with the commission, "Go ye into all the world and preach the Gospel to every creature." The Lord has given languages to the unlearned, Greek, Latin, Hebrew, French, German, Italian, Chinese, Japanese, Zulu and languages of Africa, Hindu and Bengali and dialects of India, Chippewa and other languages of the Indians, Esquimaux, the deaf mute language and, in fact the Holy Ghost speaks all the languages of the world through His children.

A minister says that God showed him twenty years ago that the divine plan for missionaries was that they might receive the gift of tongues either before going to the foreign field or on the way. It should be a sign to the heathen that the message is of God. The gift of tongues can only be used as the Spirit gives utterance. It cannot be learned like the native tongue, but the Lord takes control of the organs of speech at will. It is emphatically, God's message.

During a meeting at Monrovia, a preacher who at one time had been used of God in the Pentecost Bands under Vivian Dake, but had cooled off, was reclaimed, sanctified and filled with the Holy Ghost. When the power of God came on him, his eight-year-old son was kneeling behind him. The boy had previously sought and obtained a clear heart, and when the Holy Ghost fell on his father, He also fell on him and his hands began to shake and he sang in tongues.

Bro. Campbell, a Nazarene brother, 83 years of age, who has been for 53 years serving the Lord, received the baptism with the Holy Ghost and gift of tongues in his own home. His son, who was a physician, was called and came to see if he was sick, but found him only happy in the Lord. Not only old men and old women, but boys and girls, are receiving their Pentecost. Viola Price, a little orphan colored girl eight years of age, has received the gift of tongues.

Mrs. Lucy F. Farrow, God's anointed handmaid, who came some four months ago from Houston, Texas, to Los Angeles, bringing this full Gospel, and whom God has greatly used as she laid her hands on many who have received the Pentecost and the gift of tongues, has now returned to Houston, en route to Norfolk, Va. This is her old home which she left as a girl, being sold into slavery in the south. The Lord, she feels, is now calling her back. Sister Farrow, Bro. W. J. Seymour and Bro. J. A. Warren were the three that the Lord sent from Houston as messengers of the full gospel.

THE APOSTOLIC FAITH MOVEMENT

Stands for the restoration of the faith once delivered unto the saints—the old time religion, camp meetings, revivals, missions, street and prison work and Christian Unity everywhere.

Teaching on Repentance—Mark 1:14, 15.

Godly Sorrow for Sin, Example—Matt. 9:13; 2 Cor. 7, 9, 11; Acts 3:19; Acts 17:30, 31.

Of Confession of Sins—Luke 15:21 and Luke 18:13.

Forsaking Sinful Ways—Isa. 55:7; Jonah 3:8; Prov. 28; 13.

Restitution—Ezek. 33;15; Luke 19:8.

And faith in Jesus Christ.

First Work—Justification is that act of God's free grace by which we receive remission of sins. Acts 10:42, 43; Rom. 3:25.

Second Work—Sanctification is the second work of grace and the last work of grace. Sanc-

tification is that act of God's free grace by which He makes us holy. John 17:15, 17—"Sanctify them through Thy Truth; Thy word is truth." 1 Thess. 4:3; 1 Thess. 5:23; Heb. 13:12; Heb. 2:11; Heb. 12:14.

Sanctification is cleansing to make holy. The Disciples were sanctified before the Day of Pentecost. By a careful study of Scripture you will find it is so now. "Ye are clean through the word which I have spoken unto you" (John 15:3; 13:10); and Jesus had breathed on them the Holy Ghost (John 20:21, 22). You know, that they could not receive the Spirit if they were not clean. Jesus cleansed and got all doubt out of His Church before He went back to glory.

The Baptism with the Holy Ghost is a gift of power upon the sanctified life; so when we get it we have the same evidence as the Disciples received on the Day of Pentecost (Acts 2:3, 4), in speaking in new tongues. See also Acts 10:45, 45; Acts 19:6; 1 Cor. 14:21. "For I will work a work in your days which ye will not believe though it be told you."—Hab. 1:5

Seeking Healing—He must believe that God is able to heal.—Ex. 15:26: "I am the Lord that healeth thee." James 5:14; Psa. 103:3; 2 Kings 20:5; Matt. 8:16, 17; Mark 16; 16, 17, 18.

He must believe God is able to heal. "Behold I am the Lord, the God of all flesh; is there any thing too hard for Me?"—Jer. 32:27

Too many have confused the grace of Sanctification with the enduement of Power, or the Baptism with the Holy Ghost; others have taken "the anointing that abideth" for the Baptism, and failed to reach the glory and power of a true Pentecost.

The blood of Jesus will never blot out any sin between man and man they can make right; but if we can't make wrongs right the Blood graciously covers. (Matt. 5:23, 24.)

We are not fighting men or churches, but seeking to displace dead forms and creeds and wild fanaticisms with living, practical Christi-anity. "Love, Faith, Unity" are our watchwords, and "Victory through the Atoning Blood" our battle cry. God's promises are true. He said: "Be thou faithful over a few things, and I will make thee ruler over many." From the little handful of Christians who stood by the cross when the testings and discouragements came, God has raised a mighty host.

Two

THE PENTECOSTAL BAPTISM RESTORED, OCTOBER 1906

THE APOSTOLIC FAITH

"Earnestly contend for the faith which was once delivered unto the saints."—Jude 3

Vol. 1, No. 2   Los Angeles, Cal., October, 1906   Subscription Free

THE PROMISED LATTER RAIN NOW BEING POURED OUT ON GOD'S HUMBLE PEOPLE

All along the ages men have been preaching a partial Gospel. A part of the Gospel remained when the world went into the dark ages. God has from time to time raised up men to bring back the truth to the church. He raised up Luther to bring back to the world the doctrine of justification by faith. He raised up another reformer in John Wesley to establish Bible holiness in the church. Then he raised Dr. Cullis who brought back to the world the wonderful doctrine of divine healing. Now He is bringing back the Pentecostal Baptism to the church.

God laid His hand on a little crippled boy seven years of age and healed him of disease and made him whole except his ankles. He walked on the sides of his ankles. Then, when he was fourteen years of age, he had been sent to college and God had called him to preach. One day as he was sitting reading his Bible, a man came for him to go and hold a meeting. He began to say to the Lord: "Father, if I go to that place, it will be necessary for me to walk here and yonder. Just put strength into these ankle joints of mine." And immediately he was made whole and leaped and praised God, like the man at the beautiful gate. He has since been in evangelistic work over the United States, seeing multitudes saved, sanctified and healed.

Five years ago, God put it into this man's heart (Bro. Charles Parham) to go over to Topeka, Kansas, to educate missionaries to carry the Gospel. It was a faith

21

school and the Bible was the only textbook. The students had gathered there without tuition or board, God sending in the means to carry on the work. Most of the students had been religious workers and said they had received the baptism with the Holy Ghost a number of years ago. Bro. Parham became convinced that there was no religious school that tallied up with the second chapter of Acts. Just before the first of January, 1901, the Bible School began to study the word on the Baptism with the Holy Ghost to discover the Bible evidence of this baptism that they might obtain it.

The students kept up continued prayer in the praying tower. A company would go up and stay three hours, and then another company would go up and wait on God praying that all the promises of the Word might be wrought out in their lives.

On New Year's night, Miss Agnes N. Ozman, one who had had for years "the anointing that abideth," which she mistook for the baptism, was convinced of the need for a personal Pentecost. A few minutes before midnight, she desired hands laid on her that she might receive the gift of the Holy Ghost. During prayer and invocation of hands, she was filled with the Holy Ghost and spake with other tongues as the Spirit gave utterance.

This made all hungry. Scarcely eating or sleeping, the school with one accord waited on God. On the 3rd of January, 1901, Bro. Parham being absent holding a meeting at the time, while they all waited on God to send the baptism of the Spirit, suddenly twelve students were filled with the Holy Ghost and began to speak with other tongues, and when Bro. Parham returned and opened the door of the room where they were gathered, a wonderful sight met his eyes. The whole room was filled with a white sheen of light that could not be described, and twelve of the students were on their feet talking in different languages.

He said they seemed to pay no attention at all to him, and

he knelt in one corner and said: "O, God, what does this mean?" The Lord said: "Are you able to stand for the experience in the face of persecution and howling mobs?" He said: "Yes, Lord, if you will give me the experience, for the laborer must first be partaker of the fruits." Instantly the Lord took his vocal organs, and he was preaching the Word in another language.

This man has preached in different languages over the United States, and men and women of that nationality have come to the altar and sought God. He was surely raised up of God to be an apostle of the doctrine of Pentecost.

This Pentecostal Gospel has been spreading ever since, but on the Pacific coast it has burst out in great power and is being carried from here over the world. We are expecting Bro. Parham to visit Los Angeles in a few days and for a mightier tide of salvation to break out.

FIRE STILL FALLING

The waves of Pentecostal salvation are still rolling in at Azusa Street Mission. From morning till late at night the meetings continue with about three altar services a day. We have made no record of souls saved, sanctified and baptized with the Holy Ghost, but a brother said last week he counted about fifty in all that had been baptized with the Holy Ghost during the week. Then at Eighth Street and Maple Avenue, the People's church, Monrovia, Whittier, Hermon, Sawtelle, Pasadena, Elysian Heights, and other places the work is going on and souls are coming through amid great rejoicing.

Four of the Holiness preachers have received the baptism with the Holy Ghost. One of them, Bro. Wm. Pendleton, with his congregation, being turned out of the church, are holding meetings at Eighth Street and Maple Avenue. There is a heavenly atmosphere there. The altar is filled with seekers, people are slain under the power of God, and rising in a life baptized with the Holy Ghost.

The fire is spreading. People are writing from different

points to know about this Pentecost, and are beginning to wait on God for their Pentecost. He is no respecter of persons and places. We expect to see a wave of salvation go over this world. While this work has been going on for five years, it has burst out in great power on this coast. There is power in the full Gospel. Nothing can quench it.

Missionaries for the foreign fields, equipped with several languages, are now on their way and others are only waiting for the way to open and for the Lord to say: "Go." We are on our faces before God. Let a volume of prayer go up from all the Lord's people. Awake! Awake! There is but time to dress and be ready, for the cry will soon go forth. "The Bridegroom cometh."

Eight missionaries have started to the foreign field since this movement began in Lost Angeles a few months ago. About thirty workers have gone out into the field.

The brother at Elysian Heights who received his eyesight after being blind for a year and a half, is a living witness of the power of God. Since that he has been sanctified and anointed with the Holy Ghost, and his wife has been saved.

In the City of Oakland, during the five weeks that the band from Los Angeles was there, Brother and Sister Evans and Sister Florence Crawford, sixty-five souls received the baptism with the Holy Ghost, thirty were sanctified and nineteen converted.

A man who was twice in the insane asylum, an infidel that had been going from place to place denying the name of Jesus Christ, is now saved, sanctified and baptized with the Holy Ghost, and working to win others.

Sometimes, among officers of the law, we find a keen judgment in regard to genuine or spurious religion. In Pasadena, where the Lord was working in power some months ago, the chief of police made the remark: "I would not give much for a meeting that did not have a shout in it."

Sister Lizzie Frazer of Colorado Springs, Colorado, was one of those who received the gift of tongues when the Palestine Missionary band passed through there. She writes that she expects to go to India with a band of missionaries next month. The Lord has given her a wonderful equipment.

Mrs. J. Kring was healed of cancer of the lungs on August 8, after the doctor had given her up. One lung was entirely closed up. When she was prayed for, the Lord immediately touched her body and healed her. She shouted for an hour with strong lungs, and is the happiest woman you ever saw.

A woman brought her son to the Mission to be healed of epileptic fits. He is about twenty-one years old and has been suffering for years, like the boy that was brought to Jesus whom the devil had often caused to fall into the fire and into the water. The boy was so wrecked in mind and body that he was in a semi-conscious condition. Bro. Batman, who is called to Africa, prayed for him, asking the Lord to cast the demon power out of him and give complete healing. The boy raised up from the floor and witnessed that the work was done and went home rejoicing.

A brother living in the east had been sick for quite a while and sent a handkerchief to be blessed as in Bible times. His sister brought it to the Mission, praying for the Lord to show her to whom she was to give it, and the Lord showed her to give it to Sister Sallie Trainor. She immediately took it upstairs and as she knelt before the Lord, the Spirit came upon her in great power and she prayed in tongues, and kissed the handkerchief three times, as the Spirit seemed to lead her. It was sent with a prayer and the brother was immediately healed.

A PORTUGUESE MINISTER RECEIVES HIS PENTECOST

Rev. Adolph Rosa, a Portuguese brother from Cape Verde Islands, was baptized with the Holy Ghost in Oakland and is now in Los Angeles preaching the full Gospel. He was a Catholic and his father had expected to have him educated as a Catholic priest; but God had His hand upon him. He came to America, was converted from the power of Romanism and captivity about six years ago in a Portuguese Methodist church in New Bedford, Mass., and entered the ministry of the Methodist church as a missionary to the Portuguese in the state of California. He was sanctified about four years ago, and is now conducting Pentecostal meetings in the People's church in Los Angeles.

BRO. ROSA'S TESTIMONY

When Rev. Evans and his wife and Sister Florence Crawford went to the city of Oakland preaching the full Gospel, I went the first night, not to criticize but to investigate. Many preachers were there to criticize, but when I stepped in, I felt the power of God and could not say that it was the work of the devil, as most of the preachers declared, for I was practically convinced that it was the work of the Holy Ghost. I went home and began to study my Bible, and went to God in prayer to reveal to me if these people were really the people of God. He revealed to me in the attitude of my supplication, that they were preaching exactly what the disciples of old preached. I was convinced that every minister of the Gospel should receive the same baptism with the Holy Ghost and fire that the disciples received on the day of Pentecost, before they are prepared to preach the Gospel. I was teaching that when we received sanctification, we receive the Holy Ghost, as most of the preachers were teaching. But as I went to my Bible with the spirit of prayer, God revealed to me that the disciples were justified before Christ ascended; but they never were baptized with the Holy Ghost until the day of Pentecost.

The second day that I went to the meeting, the Lord put a real hunger in my soul to go forward, but I was too proud as a minister of the Gospel to humble myself in a lowly mission and let ladies pray over me for the gift of the Holy Ghost, and I had in my mind what people would think of me. But the third day, as I arose to testify in the audience, the only words I could say were: "What does God think of me?" Then I could only weep for some minutes and the power of God came upon me until I dropped to the floor. I was under the power of God for about an hour and a half, and it was there that all pride, and self, and conceit disappeared, and I was really dead to the world, for I had Christ within in His fullness. I was baptized with the Holy Ghost and spoke in a new tongue.

I praise God for the light, and now I am walking in it.

The desire of my heart is to see every man and woman that preaches the Gospel of Christ, baptized with the Holy Ghost, for without the Holy Ghost it is almost impossible for us to convince the world of sin, of righteousness, and the judgment.

GET INTO THE CORNFIELD

"It is an awful hard thing to get a holiness preacher that has been indoctrinated for years to see that he has not received his Pentecost. I have been preaching for twenty years and never preached anything but a full salvation. To get a fellow that has been preaching twenty years to see that he has not received the baptism, when he has been preaching all the time that he has it, and then to get him to turn seeker, is a hard job. I tell you it means for him to get pretty near the end of himself.

"The time has come, in the full blaze of Pentecost, that if you do not walk in the light, you will become a dry chip. I bless God, I humbled myself. On the 10th day of July the

Lord gave me the evidence of the Pentecost. It took me three weeks, searching the Word, from Genesis to Revelation to see that these things were so. Any fellow that will get down on his knees and pray through and read through, will find that the Holy Ghost only falls on a clean temple. You must give over and let God have His way.

"So many folks remind me of the hog that was trying to get into a big cornfield. There was a big, hollow, crooked log in the fence, laid in such a way that both ends of the log were on the same side of the fence. The hog would go into one end of the log, expecting that he would get into the cornfield. He would go in and come out, and look all around to see how it was that he was not in the cornfield. There are a lot of folks today just in that place. They crawl through a hollow log of experience and never get anything. Bless God, I would hunt the way. Jesus said: 'I am the way.' Get into the cornfield. Hunt for the wicket gate and you will get in. Hallelu-

jah! I am in the cornfield."

The above is the testimony of Bro. Hill, a Nazarene preacher. He and his wife have both received their personal Pentecost and Bible evidence.

TESTIMONIES OF OUT-GOING MISSIONARIES

A company of three missionaries left Los Angeles September 13, en route for the west coast of Africa. Sister Hutchins has been preaching the Gospel in the power of the Spirit. She has received the baptism with the Holy Ghost and the gift of the Uganda language, the language of the people to whom she is sent. A brother who has been in that country understands and has interpreted the language she speaks. Her husband is with her and her niece, who also has been given the African language.

SISTER HUTCHINS' TESTIMONY

I was justified on the 4th of July, 1901, and at that time, I felt the Lord wanted me in Africa, but I was not then at all willing to go. But on the 28th of July, 1903, the Lord sanctified me. Before He sanctified me, He asked me if I would go to Africa. I promised Him I would. From that time on, I have felt the call to Africa, but not knowing just when the Lord would have me leave.

On the sixth of last month, while out in my back yard one afternoon, I heard a voice speaking to me these words: "On the 15th day of September, take your husband and baby and start out for Africa." And I looked around and about me to see if there was not someone speaking to me, but I did not see anyone, and I soon recognized that it was the voice of God. I looked up into the heavens and said: "Lord, I will obey." Since then I have had many tests and temptations from the devil. He has at times told me that I would not even live to see the 15th of September, but I never once doubted God. I knew that He was able to bring everything to pass that He told me to do.

After hearing the voice telling me to leave Los Angeles on the 15th, I went to one of my neighbors and testified to

her that the Lord had told me to leave for Africa on the 15th of September. She looked at me with a smile. I asked her what she was smiling about. She said: "Because you have not got street car fare to go to Azusa Street Mission tonight, and talking about going to Africa." But I told her I was trusting in a God that could bring all things to pass that He wanted us to do. He has really supplied all my needs in every way, for the work where He has called me.

I want to testify also about my husband. He was a backslider, and how the devil did test me, saying: "You are going out to cast the devil out of others, and going to take a devil with you." My husband was not saved, but I held on to God and said: "Lord, I will obey."

I continued to testify and to make preparations to leave on the 15th. The Lord reclaimed my husband and sanctified him wholly and put the glory and shout in him. So now it is my time to laugh. The devil has oppressed and mocked me;

but praise the Lord, now I can mock him. Glory to God!

It is now ten minutes to four o'clock in the afternoon on the 15th day of September. I am all ready and down to the Mission with my ticket and everything prepared, waiting to have hands laid on and the prayers of the saints, and expect to leave at eight o'clock from the Santa Fe station en route for Africa. We expect to go to Mt. Coffee, Monrovia, Liberia.

Feeling the need of a real companion in the Gospel that was out and out for God, I prayed to God that He might give me one to go with me. I had my eyes upon one that I wanted to go, but in prayer and humility before God, I found out it was not the one the Lord wanted to go. So I said: "Anyone, Lord, that you would have to go will be pleasing to me." And, to my surprise, He gave me my niece—a girl that I had raised from a child. Now she is nineteen years of age, is saved, sanctified and baptized with the Holy Ghost, and is going with me out into the work of the Lord. So instead of giving me one companion, He gave me two—my niece and my husband.

Our first step will be Chattanooga, Tenn., Harge Row. I want the prayers of the saints that I may stay humble. —Mrs. J. W. Hutchins, Mt. Coffee, Monrovia, Liberia, Africa

A GIRL'S CONSECRATION FOR AFRICA

I am saved, sanctified and baptized with the Holy Ghost and have the Bible evidence. The Lord showed me that the language I spoke was the language of Africa. My aunt who has been the same as a mother to me, was going to Africa. I asked the Lord if He wanted me to go, to open up a way for me, and the next morning He opened the way for me. I did not have the means and He gave me the fare and supplied all my needs. I am willing to trust Him through to Africa. I know the Lord wants me to go there. I want to testify to those people and teach the children about the blessed Lord, and to work for the Lord. I am willing to forsake all my loved ones for His sake. I want the saints to pray for me for I am young in the Lord.—Leila McKinney

PENTECOSTAL SCENES

At Brunner, Texas, in August, a wonderful meeting was held by the Apostolic Faith people. Fifty, seventy-five, and one hundred seekers at a service crowded the altars for two whole weeks. The sixty-foot altar was doubled half way back, then trebled, until the whole front half of the Tabernacle was occupied with the great altar service. Think of one hundred seekers and twice as many faithful Christians assisting, all praying before God. Glory to His great name! Then see them rise with shining faces and Pentecostal power.

CAME THREE HUNDRED MILES

Some have come long distances to see the Pentecost in Los Angeles. An Armenian brother, who came three hundred miles, said, "I am like the queen of Sheba who went to see the wisdom of Solomon, only when I heard about these meetings, I did not come so far, I came only 300 miles to see if this was true. And now I am well satisfied that I see the wonderful works of God. If these people who have only a few drops from God are crazy, what will it be when the shower comes. The shower follows the drops."

UNITED TO JESUS

Jesus says, "Take my yoke upon you and learn of me." The Lord showed me that this yoke was the covenant of the new testament in His blood, and we put this yoke on when we are baptized with the Holy Ghost. This covenant is a marriage covenant. We are married, not for one day or year or life, but eternally married. When I got married to my wife it was settled for this life. So when I got married to Jesus Christ, it was settled forever. Hallelujah! Jesus and I are united. He baptized me with love.

THE WORK IN VIRGINIA
907 Glasken St.,
Portsmouth, Va.

We had a glorious meeting last night. It was the sixth night and we have six speaking in tongues. It is wonderful to see how the Lord is working with His believing children, but there is much to be done here. There is a band of saints that do not read the Bible like saints. They say the Bible is for unbelievers so they do not read it at all. O for someone to help. Won't you come and help if you can, and as soon as you can?

God is making a short work in the earth today. He is soon coming to earth again. He said we should not get over the cities until the Son of Man should come, so we have not much time to lose. Remember me to all of the saints. Tell them to pray for me much. I can't write to all, so you remember me to all as one. Ask them to pray for the work in Virginia. It is much needed. I don't know how long the Lord is going to keep me here. There is so much to be done.

I did not come through Danville, but I am going there as soon as I can get off from this place. I came through New Orleans and changed cars there, and laid hands on two sick, and sowed seed on the way from Houston here. —Lucy Farrow

A later report is that twenty have received the baptism of the Holy Ghost in Portsmouth.

CHINESE WANT THE GOSPEL OF THE BIBLE

A dear friend went to China as a surgical missionary, preaching the Gospel and cutting up people. She has been in China eight years and only has a little of the language. (Cannot God, who confounded the people at the tower of Babel, and caused all nations at Jerusalem to hear in their own tongue, give a language?) She writes that the Chinese are smart people, and some of them had been reading the Bible and came to her with the open Book, saying, "When you do what your God tells you, then we will believe in your God. Here He says, 'These signs shall follow them that believe, they shall lay hands on the sick and they shall recover,' And here you come with your knives cutting us up, and with your pill bags. Why don't you do what your God tells you to do?" What do these things mean? They mean that if we go as representatives of our Lord, we must go with the equipment He gives. The heathen want the whole Gospel.

LITTLE CHILDREN RE-CEIVE THE HOLY GHOST

A number of children have been baptised with the Holy Ghost. A sister at Hermon has been holding a daily children's meeting and there children have been baptised with the Holy Ghost. One Sunday night also at Azusa Street Mission three little girls, sisters, were baptized with the Holy Ghost and each of them spoke in tongues, and different languages. It was touching to see how they went to praying for others at the altar. They had to leave with their mother for Canada and expect to cross the ocean from there, but before they left the Lord gave them their Pentecost. A number of children have been clearly saved and sancti-fied in the Sunday afternoon children's meeting, led by the boy preacher, Clayborn, on Sunday afternoons and some have received the gift of the Holy Ghost, and God is using their testimonies.

Apostolic power will mean apostolic persecution. Hell with all its power will be turned lose. It behooves us to get a spiritual backbone, spiritual stamina and stick-to-it-iveness that will enable us to stand in these last days against all the forces of the enemy. Jesus came to destroy all the works of the devil, and He said He would give us power, the Holy Ghost coming upon us, the same power that He had.

William Seymour preached regularly at the Azusa Street Revival

Three

BIBLE PENTECOST, NOVEMBER 1906

THE APOSTOLIC FAITH

"Earnestly contend for the faith which was once delivered unto the saints."—Jude 3

Vol. 1, No. 3, Los Angeles, Cal., November, 1906, Subscription Free

GRACIOUS PENTECOSTAL SHOWERS CONTINUE TO FALL

The news has spread far and wide that Los Angeles is being visited with a "rushing mighty wind from heaven." The how and why of it is to be found in the very opposite of those conditions that are usually thought necessary for a big revival. No instruments of music are used, none are needed. No choir—but bands of angels have been heard by some in the spirit and there is a heavenly singing that is inspired by the Holy Ghost. No collections are taken. No bills have been posted to advertise the meetings. No church or organization is back of it. All who are in touch with God realize as soon as they enter the meetings that the Holy Ghost is the leader. One brother states that even before his train entered the city, he felt the power of the revival.

Travelers from afar wend their way to the headquarters at Azusa Street. As they enquire their way to the Apostolic Faith Mission, perhaps they are asked, "O, you mean the Holy Rollers," or "Is it the Colored Church you mean?" In the vicinity of a tombstone shop, stables and lumber yard (a fortunate vicinity because no one complains of all-night meetings) you find a two-story, white-washed old building. You would hardly expect heavenly visitations there, unless you remember the stable at Bethlehem.

But here you find a mighty pentecostal revival going on from ten o'clock in the morning till about twelve at night. Yes, Pentecost has come to hundreds of hearts and many homes are made into a sweet paradise below. We remember years ago, when a bright, young missionary was dying in Bombay, India, in his last hours, unconscious with the fever, he kept crying, "Pentecost is coming! Pentecost is coming!" It seemed prophetical. Pentecost has come and is coming in India, and thank God in many other places.

A leading Methodist layman of Los Angeles says, "Scenes transpiring here are what Los Angeles churches have been praying for for years. I have been a Methodist for twenty-five years. I was a leader of the praying band of the First Methodist Church. We prayed that the Pentecost might come to the city of Los Angeles. We wanted it to start in the First Methodist Church, but God did not start it there. I bless God that it did not start in any church in this city, but in a barn, so that we might all come and take part in it. If it had been started in a fine church, poor colored people and Spanish people would not have got it, but praise God it

started here. God Almighty says He will pour out of His Spirit upon all flesh. This is just what is happening here. I want to warn every Methodist in Los Angeles to keep your hands off this work. Tell the people wherever you go that Pentecost has come to Los Angeles."

As soon as it is announced that the altar is open for seekers for pardon, sanctification, the baptism with the Holy Ghost and healing of the body, the people rise and flock to the altar. There is no urging. What kind of preaching is it that brings them? Why, the simple declaring of the Word of God. There is such power in the preaching of the Word in the Spirit that people are shaken on the benches. Coming to the altar, many fall prostrate under the power of God, and often come out speaking in tongues. Sometimes the power falls on people and they are wrought upon by the Spirit during testimony or preaching and receive Bible experiences.

The testimony meetings which precede the preaching

often continue for two hours or more and people are standing waiting to testify all the time. Those who have received the baptism with the Holy Ghost testify that they had a clear evidence of sanctification first. Hundreds testify that they received the Bible evidence of speaking in a new tongue that they never knew before. Some have received the "gift of tongues" or "divers tongues" and the interpretation.

The demonstrations are not the shouting, clapping or jumping so often seen in camp meetings. There is a shaking such as the early Quakers had and which the old Methodists called the "jerks." It is while under the power of the Spirit you see the hands raised and hear speaking in tongues. While one sings a song learned from heaven with a shining face, the tears will be trickling down other faces. Many receive the Spirit through the laying on of hands, as they did through Paul at Ephesus.

Little children from eight years to twelve stand up on the altar bench and testify to the baptism with the Holy Ghost and speak in tongues. In the children's meetings little tots get down and seek the Lord.

It is noticeable how free all nationalities feel. If a Mexican or German cannot speak English, he gets up and speaks in his own tongue and feels quite at home for the Spirit interprets through the face and people say amen. No instrument that God can use is rejected on account of color or dress or lack of education. This is why God has so built up the work.

In the testimony meetings, they report from cottage prayer meetings where perhaps a number were baptized with the Holy Ghost or saved or sanctified and those who have been seeking at home report what God has done for them.

The singing is characterized by freedom. "The Comforter Has Come" is sung every day, also "Heavenly Sunlight" and "Under the Blood." Often one will rise and sing a familiar song in a new tongue.

Seekers for healing are

usually taken upstairs and prayed for in the prayer room and many have been healed there. There is a larger room upstairs that is used for Bible study. A brother fittingly describes it in this way, "Upstairs is a long room, furnished with chairs and three California redwood planks, laid end to end on backless chairs. This is the Pentecostal upper room where sanctified souls seek Pentecostal fullness and go out speaking in new tongues."

The sweetest thing of all is the loving harmony. Every church where this has gone is like a part of the family. This description is given for the benefit of the many friends who write in and who would like to be present. So many letters are received in the Apostolic Faith office, which is in the same building as the mission. We cannot but weep as we read these letters and pray for those who are seeking.

The Lord is saving drunkards and taking the appetite for liquor and tobacco completely away.

Reports come from Denver that forty souls have received the Pentecost and are speaking in tongues.

A young man saved from the morphine habit has no more desire for the stuff and gave up his instruments.

Four workers from Texas, Bro. and Sister Oyler and Bro. and Sister Quinton have arrived in Los Angeles lately. God has been using them in Whittier.

Bro. Tom Qualls from Fresno said, "I came 300 miles to this meeting and I feel heaven in my soul. It seems to me I am getting some of the crumbs that fall from the Father's table. I feel the presence of God here."

"Cartoons in the newspapers were my first introduction to this meeting," said a brother, "and I said, this is what I have been praying for for years. I was warned by leaders that it was of the devil, but I came and got a touch of heaven in my soul."

Before the fire broke out in Los Angeles a brother had a vision of fires springing up and then gathering together and advancing in a solid wall of flame. A preacher was trying to put it out with a wet gunny sack, but it was evident there was no use fighting it. Our God is marching on. Hallelujah. The man with the wet gunny sack is here also, but his efforts only call attention to the fire.

The blind man who was saved and had his sight restored was saved because of hearing a few praying in tongues in a cottage meeting. He was a sinner; a very profane man, and was convicted because of tongues. Praise God for His marvelous works to the children of men.

Sister Lemon of Whittier, who had been a sufferer for eighteen years and could receive no help from physicians, and had been bed-ridden for fourteen years of that time, has been marvelously healed by the Lord through the laying on of hands and the prayer of faith. She has been walking to meetings. The opposers of the work cannot deny that a notable miracle has been performed through the mighty name of Jesus.

Mother Griffith, who has been matron of a rescue home, has received her Pentecost. She testified, "It seemed to me when I got saved, I got into the ocean; and when I got sanctified, it seemed the ocean got into me; and when I was baptized with the Holy Ghost, it seemed I got the life preserver on and began floating on the ocean of salvation. Jesus lives in me, and I live and have my being in Him. Thank God for salvation, sanctification, the baptism with the Holy Ghost and the witness."

Sister Bridget Welch has been powerfully baptized with the Holy Ghost and is working for the Lord both in laboring for souls and in service with her hands ministering to others. She testifies, "I was a dope fiend and in and out of prisons for twenty years. God Almighty has surely healed my body and given me divine strength. He healed me of cancer of the nose and did not leave a scar. I have no time for a drugstore anymore. The Lord took me out of an awful pit and set my feet on the solid rock and established my goings and put a new song in my mouth. He sanctified me and baptized me with the Holy Ghost and gave me the gift of tongues."

A sister who was very hungry for the Pentecost prayed for the Lord to strip her of everything, but give more of Himself. Then shortly afterwards when her house was in flames, she went out and knelt down in the weeds and prayed, "Lord, you said all things work together for good to them that love you. Give me more of God." And He answered prayer and gave her a mighty baptism with the Holy Ghost and fire and she is shining for God.

PENTECOST IN DENVER
1934 E. 18th Ave., Denver, Colo.

What I received on that memorable Sunday night in Los Angeles has never left me for one moment and last night in particular at the meeting, did the Holy Ghost magnify the simple Gospel of our Lord in demonstration and power, until about twenty-five crowded the altar and got definite experiences of justification, sanctification, baptism with the Holy Ghost, and healing. One dear old man, who because of his back, could not straighten up nor stoop down without severe pain, was instantly healed, got up and showed the people how the dear Lord had healed him. He stood as straight as a young man, stooped down, touched the floor with his hands without a bit of pain. Then he knelt down and said, "I want the baptism with the Holy Ghost," and Glory to God, he got it, and there was great joy.

Dear Bro. Seymour, God surely sent me here. These dear, hungry people, when they learned I came from the meeting at Los Angeles, received me with open arms. They gave me the evening, and during the meeting, they embraced me and our joy in the Lord knew no bounds. One dear brother from Los Angeles picked me up and held me as if I were a child. This is but the beginning of a work here such as we knew in Los Angeles. This people have been praying that God would send someone to teach them and give them light and wisdom, and they believe God has answered their prayers, hence their great joy. I feel the need of your prayers. I never saw in all my travels a people so hungry for the truth.

Dear Bro. G. F. Fink, the brother in charge, was coming to Los Angeles to Azusa Street to learn and get a better understanding of the baptism with the Holy Ghost. While I was talking to the people last night, he arose and embraced me crying, I love you, I love you, my brother. Surely God has sent you to us; and the people wept for joy, and shouted praises unto God. These people here were set on fire by the Holy Ghost through Bro. Johnson and the two sisters who passed through here, and it is marvelous how the Holy Ghost has led them. You little know how the people have been praying for you and the meetings in Los Angeles in the midst of their own struggles. Give my love in Jesus to all the saints.—T. Hazmalhalch

VICTORY IN OAKLAND

Bro. Harmon Clifford, the young man who was saved, sanctified, and baptized with the Holy Ghost, all in an hour and a half at the Azusa Street Mission, and who was also healed of consumption, has been increasing in power, and God has bestowed on him many gifts. He writes from Oakland where the Lord sent him.

"How I praise God for ever sending me to Oakland with Bro. Rosa. I was never so happy in all my life as I have been this last week. It did seem as though I would go up at any moment, but of course God has a work for me to do yet. Praise His dear name. There was some trouble about the Bible evidence to the baptism with the Holy Ghost, but as soon as that was straight, God began to work and has been working ever since. O glory to God! Many have been saved, sanctified, and healed. Six have received Pentecost and spoke in a good, clear language up to Thursday night. People were laid out all over the mission. The people have been very quiet and let the Holy Ghost have right of way, and sometimes before the preaching is over people come to the altar. There are many hungry souls in this city."— 336 Ninth St., Oakland, Ca.

VISION AND MESSAGE

A sister who has been healed and baptized with the Holy Ghost related the following vision, "Two days ago the power of God came over me and He said, 'Whatsoever ye ask in my name believing, ye shall receive.' Immediately I was in a great hall with tables spread all about, and the Lord was the waiter, and I saw His beautiful, smiling face. He spoke to me and said, 'I have called my friends and they did not come, therefore go out and ask everyone you find to come to the wedding.' As I looked around to see something beautiful, the scene changed and I was in a hospital and saw poor creatures dying, looking like skeletons. I thought my call was to the hospital and telephoned to know when it was open for visitors, but the Lord revealed to me that it meant all those who are sick in their souls."

A CORRECTION

In our last issue, there was a prophecy by Sister Mary Golmond of an earthquake coming to Los Angeles. She stated that the Lord had not showed the time, but that it would NOT come on Sunday. The word "not" was accidentally omitted.

HIS BANQUETING HOUSE

"He took me into his banqueting house, and his banner over me was love." A brother says the Lord gave him a vision of the banqueting house. He passed under the great arches. Each one had a name upon it.

The first was love, then there was joy, peace, and among others he saw, "Independence." He asked what that meant. The answer was, "Is it not wonderful to be free?" Dear saints, this is one of the sweetest arches in the banqueting house. This bondage to love sets me perfectly free.

UNUSUAL NOISE

There has been some unusual noise in the town of Whittier, the prayers of those who are burdened for the lost, the sound of praises to God and speaking in new tongues. A few days ago, four workers were arrested while praying in the cottage that had been offered free of rent for the use of the workers. The following letter was received at Azusa Street.

"Bro. Seymour in Jesus: We are charged with using boisterous language, unusual noise, or in other words praising God and speaking in tongues. This happened in the cottage this morning. The defendants are Sister May Mayo, Sister Jacobson, Bro. and Sister McLain. Trial comes off at 4 p. m. We are standing steadfast, seeing the glory of God. We believe the judge is under conviction. Sunday night nine souls were at the altar. Souls getting saved and sanctified. Power is falling in the audience. People being slain."

When the word came to Azusa Street, fifteen workers rallied to take the place of the four and meetings have been going on there with victory and power ever since.

The band that were arrested are rejoicing in the Lord that they were permitted to go through the trial. The judge gave them the choice of leaving town or going to jail. They consulted the Lord about it and He said: "When they persecute in one city, flee ye to another." So the sisters obeyed but Bro. McLain preferred to stand a few days in jail and working on the chain gang. When the judge gave sentence, Sister Mayo raised her hands to heaven and prayed for him and for Whittier.

PENTECOST IN INDIA

News comes from India that the baptism with the Holy

Ghost and gift of tongues is being received there by natives who are simply taught of God. The India Alliance says, "Some of the gifts which have been scarcely heard of in the church for many centuries, are now being given by the Holy Ghost to simple, unlearned members of the body of Christ, and communities are being stirred and transformed by the wonderful grace of God. Healing, the gift of tongues, visions, and dreams, discernment of spirits, the power to prophecy and to pray the prayer of faith, all have a place in the present revival." Hallelujah! God is sending the Pentecost to India. He is no respector of persons.

VERNON MISSION

Bro. and Sister F. E. Hill are now conducting meetings at Forty-third and Forty-fourth Streets, 4307 Central Avenue. Since they received their Pentecost, they have been holding cottage meetings at their home with seekers every night. Then they told the people God had showed them to start a meeting in that section and in about

five minutes the rent was paid for the hall in advance. Bro. Hill has dropped his business and is giving all his time to Gospel work. The Nazarene Church forbade speaking in tongues or testifying on the line of the baptism with the Holy Ghost upon the sanctified life, so they with others have walked out with the Bible and the Spirit, and God is giving them souls. There is room for Spirit filled workers everywhere.

SPREADING THE FULL GOSPEL

A number of Spirit filled workers have been going out of late. Bro. Adolph Rosa and Bro. Harmon Clifford went to Oakland and God has been using them there. Then a band of seven left on the steamer for the north, for Oakland, Salem and Seattle. They were, Sister Florence Crawford, Bro. and Sister G. W. Evans, Bro. and Sister Thomas Junk, Sister Ophelia Wiley and Sister Lulu Miller. Bro. Post went to Santa Barbara, Bro. T. Hezmalhalch to Denver, Sister Potter and Violet Price to Fresno, Bro.

F. W. Williams to Alabama a Spanish brother, Brigido Perez, to San Diego. Sister Elsie Robinson to Onawa, Michigan. Bro. Seymour has been called for a short time to Oakland, but expects soon to return to headquarters at Los Angeles. We wish to keep track of the workers in the field and be united together in prayer for each other and the work in the different fields.

BAPTIZED ON A FRUIT WAGON

Bro. G. Zigler, who runs a fruit wagon, driving into Los Angeles early in the morning, says, "I was on my wagon coming down to the market praising God, when the Lord covered me with His power and I began to sing such a sweet song I had never sung anything like before. I was riding along at three o'clock in the morning. All at once I commenced to talk in a new tongue, and it was the most wonderful blessing I have ever received. What He has done for me, He will do for everybody."

The meetings have been going on now for about six months at Azusa Street day and night. How long are they going to continue? We expect them to keep on till Jesus comes, by the grace of God.

The religion of Jesus Christ is no more popular now than it was when Jesus was here. Many are rejecting the truth and are not going to receive it. The word not only says that signs shall follow them that believe, but that "They that live godly in Christ Jesus shall suffer persecution." This also is being fulfilled.

VISIONS OF JESUS

When Brother G. W. Evans was with us in Oakland, exhorting the people to come to Christ, we observed he was speaking in verse with great earnestness, in which the great blessing of salvation and happiness and eternal life were held out to all who would come to Christ and obey Him. After speaking in this manner for probably five minutes he fell backward to the floor, and remained in an unconscious state for probably ten minutes; and then arose.

Later I talked to him about this experience, and he stated that he had never committed any such verses to memory and knew nothing of having repeated them in the meeting.

He then told me that while he was speaking the whole rear end of the Hall became filled with faces of angelic beings from floor to ceiling and from wall to wall. A literal bank of beautiful faces, with Jesus in the center, and all faces turned towards Him.

He says he recognized Peter and James and John, also John Wesley.

During his gaze at this Heavenly host he spoke unconsciously the invitations and exhortations to all to come and receive the rich blessings offered. He knew nothing of his fall, but returned to consciousness to find himself on the floor.

The same thing occurred again, about ten days later in the meeting, with this difference he did not recognize any of the faces, except Jesus, standing in the center.

At both times, he says, there were waves of spiritual power and glory coming from Jesus all over him.

I believe every one in the house felt the Divine power present, and the altar was instantly crowded with penitents.—"Household of God"

A CATHOLIC THAT RECEIVED PENTECOST

Bro. Lee, whom God so wonderfully saved from darkness and a life of sin, and baptized him with the Holy Ghost, testified, "I praise God for this old barn. This is my confession box right here. My priest was Jesus Christ. I praise God for justifying me and sanctifying me wholly, and baptizing me with the Holy Ghost. Jesus Christ is the head of my church. It was Jesus did the work for me. When the Holy Ghost comes in He speaks for Himself and sings His own songs. Friends, I did not go to college to get this language. It is the Holy Ghost that speaks. He can talk the languages of the nations. It makes no difference what judges or policemen say, this Irishman is saved by the grace of God. Glory to God. It settles a man when he gets the baptism. It gives you a sound mind. This salvation keeps me out of the saloons and jails and red light district. Jesus Christ gave his life for us that we might be saved. Glory to God for a salvation that keeps me night and day. This means persecution. Hallelujah."

PREACHING TO THE SPANISH

Bro. and Sister Lopez, Spanish people, who are filled with the Holy Ghost, are being used of God in street meetings and in helping Mexicans at the altar at Azusa Street. Bro. Brigido Perez is another young Spanish boy who has received the Pentecost. He is now in San Diego. He writes his testimony in Spanish, which being translated reads, "Through the grace of Almighty God and faith in Jesus Christ, I can testify to sanctification and the baptism with the Holy Spirit and fire of love in my heart. How good He

has been to me. On September 3rd, while I was praying, I felt in my heart that Christ our Saviour wanted me to go and testify in His precious name in different parts of the country." The Holy Ghost shines out of this brother's face.

Early Azusa Street leadership, including Seymour (center),
demonstrates the significant diversity of the revival

William Seymour and his wife, Jennie Evans (Moore)
Seymour, married May 13, 1908

Four

Pentecost With Signs Following, December 1906

The Apostolic Faith

"Earnestly contend for the faith which was once delivered unto the saints."—Jude 3

Vol. 1, No. 4, Los Angeles, Cal., December, 1906, Subscription Free

Seven Months of Pentecostal Showers, Jesus, Our Projector and Great Shepherd

Many are asking how the work in Azusa Mission started and who is the founder. The Lord was the founder and He is the Projector of this movement. A band of humble people in Los Angeles had been praying for a year or more for more power with God for the salvation of lost and suffering humanity. They did not know just what they needed, but one thing they knew, people were not getting saved and healed as they desired to see. They continued to hold cottage prayer meetings for several months.

Then they felt led of the Lord to call Bro. Seymour from Houston Texas to Los Angeles, the saints in Los Angeles sending his fare. It was as truly a call from God as when He sent His holy angel to tell Cornelius to send for Peter. He came and told them about the baptism with the Spirit, and that every afternoon at three o'clock they would pray for the endument of power. He told them he did not have the Pentecost but was seeking it and wanted all the saints to pray with him till all received their Pentecost. Some believed they had it, and others believed they did not have it because the signs were not following. Hardly anyone was getting saved.

There was a great deal of opposition, but they continued to fast and pray for the baptism with the Holy Spirit, till on April 9th the fire of God fell in a cottage on Bonnie Brae. Pentecost was poured out upon workers and saints. Three days after that, Bro. Seymour received his Pentecost.

Two who had been working with him in Houston came to Los Angeles just before Pentecost fell. They came filled with the Holy Ghost and power. One of them had received her personal Pentecost, Sister Lucy Farrow, and said the Lord had sent her to join us in holding up this precious truth. She came with love and power holding up the blood of Jesus Christ in all His fullness.

And the fire has been falling ever since. Hundreds of souls have received salvation and healing. We can truly say that the revival is still going on. The Lord God is in Los Angeles in different missions and churches in mighty power, in spite of the opposition. This revival has spread through towns about Los Angeles and through the state and over the United States in different places and across the ocean. The blood of Jesus prevails against every force and power of the enemy. Glory to God.

Some are asking if Dr. Chas. F. Parham is the leader of this movement. We can answer, no he is not the leader of this movement of Azusa Mission. We thought of having him to be our leader and so stated in our paper, before waiting on the Lord.

We can be rather hasty, especially when we are very young in the power of the Holy Spirit. We are just like a baby—full of love and were willing to accept anyone that had the baptism with the Holy Spirit as our leader. But the Lord commenced settling us down, and we saw that the Lord should be our leader. So we honor Jesus as the great Shepherd of the sheep. He is our model.

The Lord adds here daily such as should be saved, and plants them in the body to suit Himself, and all work together in harmony under the power of the Holy Spirit. There is no pope, Dowieism, or Sanfordism, but we are all little children knowing only Jesus and Him crucified. This work is carried on by the people of Los Angeles that God has united by the precious blood of our Lord Jesus Christ and the power of the Holy Spirit.

Bro. Seymour is simply a humble pastor of the flock over which the Holy Ghost has made him overseer, according to Acts 20:28, "Take heed therefore, unto yourself and to the flock over which the Holy Ghost hath made you overseer, to feed the church of God which He hath purchased with His own blood." And as missionary workers and teachers go out from this place, they have the same privilege of being pastors over the people the Lord puts them over by the Holy Spirit, and of feeding them with the pure Word of God. Each mission will be united in harmony, having its own pastor simply that the Holy Ghost shall appoint.

We believe in old time repentance, old time conversion, old time sanctification, healing of our bodies and the baptism with the Holy Ghost. We believe that God made Adam in His own image, according to Gen. 5: 1; Ps. 8: 4; and Matt. 19: 4. We do not believe in any eighth-day creation, as some have taught, and we do not believe in the annihilation of the wicked.

We stand on Bible truth without compromise. We recognize every man that honors the blood of Jesus Christ to be our brother, regardless of denomination, creed, or doctrine. But we are not willing to accept any errors, it matters not how charming and sweet they may seem to be. If they do not tally with the Word of God, we reject them.

This is the year of jubilee when God is sending the latter rain, and the refreshing times have come. He has raised up a nation in seven months' time that will preach Jesus and Him crucified in all His fullness in spite of what it costs.

"The long, long night is
        past,
The morning breaks at
        last."

It seems that God is sweeping things. He is running right over the devil here—not paying any attention to Him—saving, sanctifying, and baptizing souls, bringing them out of darkness into the marvelous light of the Son of God. Hallelujah! Glory to our God.

PENTECOST AMONG THE YOUNG PEOPLE

A band of Spirit-filled boys went down to Anaheim, a town near Los Angeles. They testified what God had done for them and it made the people hungry. The second night the altar was full. In two nights, eight were sanctified, six converted, and five received the baptism. One night at about one o'clock in the morning, the Holy Ghost spoke words in Spanish through one of the young men, and a girl who was seeking her Pentecost understand that language and joyfully interpreted it, "Keep awake, do not sleep, and I will come to thy house." This same girl in about an hour and a-half received the baptism with the Holy Ghost. The work among the children was very touching. The power of God fell the second night as at the house of Cornelius. Little children had their hands up shouting. The first to get the baptism was a little boy of ten years. He began clapping his hands and started singing "Jesus Savior, Pilot Me" in and unknown tongue in clear distinct words, also "Nearer My God to Thee." Four in the same family inside of twenty minutes got the baptism with the Holy Ghost. It was heaven there. The work is going on and other little children are being filled with the Spirit.

The band of young men that the Lord is using there and in Whittier are all in one accord and keep in the unity of the Spirit. They do not preach big sermons but simply testify and sing and pray in the Spirit. Their names are Henry Prentiss, Curtis Nichols, Orly Nichols, Tom Anderson, Wm. Millson and Isaac Berg. One night recently, seven were slain under the power of God and several received their Pentecost. Many of the people in Anaheim understand German and the workers were permitted to speak and pray in that language. Some words spoken by the Spirit in German were, "God is in our midst."

PENTECOST IN FORT WORTH

Workers went to Ft. Worth, Tex., and preached this Gospel and Pentecost has fallen there. Mrs. C. A. Roll, of 1005 Edwards Street, Ft. Worth, writes, "Three of us women began to tarry and pray the last of August. About three weeks from that time, Pentecost fell on our street. Since that time, nine have received their Pentecost. The Lord is pouring His Spirit on us. We are feeling the need of a man filled with the Holy Ghost to preach. How my heart burns within me since the Holy Ghost abides. I thank God that Pentecost has come to Ft. Worth. I just marvel at myself, by nature a timid, shrinking woman, but thank God, I am relieved of all that. We praise God for speaking to Sister Hagg and telling her to come over and help us. Then Bro. and Sister Kent came and were such a blessing to us. Two have received their Pentecost in the last few days. Others are seeking."

PENTECOST IN BENTON HARBOR

Benton Harbor, Mich., Oct. 29th

Greetings in our Lord to all the dear saints. I reached this place finding a warm welcome from Bro. and Sister York. Had our first meeting that afternoon with a room full. The meeting continued both day and night. About thirty received the message glady and searched the scriptures daily, and began to cry mightily to God for their Pentecost. After six days waiting, the fire began to fall. Now I have been here eight days and three souls have been baptized with the Holy Ghost and fire, speaking in new tongues. One young man spoke in several tongues, six or seven have received the anointing and twenty-five seeking earnestly. Victory through the blood. Hallelujah to my God. The Pentecost has come to Benton Harbor and several ministers and mission workers are among the seekers. Glory to God. He saves me and lets His power fill me. He wonderfully supplies my

needs. The battle was hot here for a time, but God gave the victory. I expect to meet you when Jesus calls us up.
—Elsie L. Robinson

PENTECOST IN SEATTLE

The Lord has been working in a marvelous way in Seattle, Wash., where Bro. and Sister Junk and Sister Lulu Miller went as workers from Los Angeles. The devil has been opposing but he always misses the mark and advertises the meetings. Five window lights were broken and one shot through and the papers call them "holy rollers," but the last reports are that some eight have been saved, ten sanctified and six received the Pentecost and are speaking in tongues. Also in a suburb town of Ballard four have received their Pentecost.

Bro. Junk writes the following incident of how God used the writing in an unknown tongue:

"The Lord sent in a young Hebrew and he got soundly converted the other night. He sobbed and cried till you could have heard him a block. His cry was for the blood to cover him. O for the old time repentance. When I pulled out my Testament to read him some Scripture, his eyes fell upon some writing I had done while under the power of God in Oakland. When he saw it, he pronounced it Hebrew. The hardest work we had to do was to convince him that I had not studied the language, but when this was clear, he trembled from head to foot and said he truly believed the Messiah was come. O glory. These signs are to them that believe not. He took my writing to a Hebrew scholar. It is Isaiah 55 commencing with the 2nd verse, Ps. 46: 3, the Lord's prayer, and Rom. 3:26. They told him not to believe me, for without studying Hebrew it would be impossible to write it, for it was perfect. Praise God, for He does only perfect work. Thos. Junk, 1617 7th Avenue, Seattle, Wash.

PENTECOST IN WOODLAND

Bro. G. W. Evans, who has just come from Woodland, California, reports a Pentecostal revival in that place. Thirty-two have been baptized with the Holy Ghost, thirty-one sanctified, and twenty saved. Seventeen members out of the Baptist Church are filled with the Holy Ghost including the superintendent of the Sunday School and his wife. The Sunday School superintendent of the Methodist Church is also baptized with the Holy Ghost, and the difficulty now on hand is the need of a larger building to accommodate the crowds. Fourteen were healed at one meeting. God's word is made so clear and plain that the crowds are pressing in spiritual hunger for the living truth. Sisters Sophie and Reece from Oakland, whom God has been using, are at present in charge.

A man that had been possessed with a mad demon and had been in the asylum was delivered. The Lord cast out this demon, clothed him in his right mind and completed the work, baptizing him with the Holy Ghost. Another remarkable case was where a party was under sentence of court, which decision was suspended and the defendant saved, sanctified, and filled with the Holy Ghost and became a good citizen.

PENTECOST IN SAN DIEGO
San Diego, Cal., Nov. 28th

We are praising God for victory in San Diego. Bro. Love and I came down here last Thursday to see if the Lord was preparing to take out a people for Himself in this city by the sea. On arriving in the city, we were not long in finding my old friend and brother, Geo. Reilly, who was earnestly tarrying for the Pentecost. We appointed a meeting at his house the same night and he was gloriously baptized with the Holy Ghost and spake with tongues. We met again the next evening and two more received their Pentecost with Bible evidence. Hallelujah! The Lord had already laid it upon Bro. Reilly to open up a mission on this line. He had secured the building and we had it ready for service by Saturday night. The people came out and nearly filled the seating capacity and we had a most wonderful meeting. Some were justified and sanctified and blessedly anointed. Interest is increasing. Some falling under the power of the Holy Ghost and mighty conviction on the people. We believe the Lord wants Azusa Street Mission duplicated in this city. We expect to stay here till the Lord says, "Flee ye to another." He has showed us that He has much people in this city. Hallelujah! Pray for us and San Diego. —F. E. Hill.

PENTECOST IN SAN JOSE

They are having a real old time Pentecostal revival in San Jose, California. The devil is stirred and doing his best to put out the fire, but they just ignore him and shout the victory. The altars are crowded day and night. Twelve have received their Pentecost and are speaking in tongues. Devils are being cast out and the sick healed. All glory to God. Some come to the altars and the Holy Ghost shows them they are backslidden in heart,

so they repent and do their first works over. Soon they get to the place where the Holy Ghost falls upon them and they rise to their feet speaking in a clear language as the Spirit gives utterance. Some of the Salvation Army people in that city are receiving the Pentecost. Bro. Harmon Clifford has returned from working in Oakland and San Jose and brings good news of a mighty work of God.

Bro. H. M. Turney, who came from Alaska to get his Pentecost in Los Angeles, is being used of the Lord in San Jose. His last report, dated November 16 is, "Yesterday was a high day in Zion. The meeting opened at 10 a.m. and was still running at one o'clock this morning. Altars are crowded at every service. Many are slain under the mighty power of God. Several received their Pentecost yesterday. One woman was instantly healed of rheumatism. Several have been saved. Many backsliders reclaimed and sanctified."

PENTECOST IN PORTSMOUTH

God has done a wonderful work in Portsmouth, Va. It is reported that about 150 have received the Pentecost. The whole country about there is stirred by the power of God. The Lord sent Sister Lucy Farrow there from Los Angeles and has been using her to preach this Gospel. She feels a call from God to go to Monrovia, Liberia, Africa, and wants someone to come and help carry on the work. She says, "Give all the saints love from me. Tell them I have many children here too. They do not want me to leave, but you all know when the Lord says go, I must go. I move as the Lord says move. No time to visit only for the Lord. I go night and day in rain and sunshine. There is no time to stop. Jesus is coming soon. Pray for me and the work here."

ANOTHER WITNESS

It pleased God by His Almighty power to send us Sister Lucy Farrow to bring us the light as we had not seen it. The power of God has fallen upon us. I praise Him for being a witness in Jerusalem, Samaria, Judea, and unto the uttermost parts of the earth. I praise Him for the power in the sign He gave me of speaking in tongues and interpreting the same and singing in tongues. I praise God for the healing power. He has healed me from my head to my feet.—Georgetta Jeffries, Portsmouth, Va.

PENTECOST IN SALEM, ORE.

We are unable to tell of the great glory and power that came upon the meetings, Sunday, November 11. With astonishment and great conviction the people witnessed the great power of another Pentecost in several speaking in tongues, and some singing songs in different languages with an unction and glory that is past human language to describe.

Waves of thrilling glory pass over me as I reflect on what God is doing in this place. A spirit of divine love prevails among the workers, and those who are baptized with the Holy Ghost take hold of the office work. Appeals for help are pouring in from every quarter, and it takes about five persons to answer the correspondence. God is raising up the workers.

People are coming and making their confessions and giving up all, to get ready for the coming of Jesus. Never in the history of this work has there been so much confession and restitution. —"Apostolic Light"

It is every believer's birthright to be baptized with the Holy Ghost.

Two bands of Apostolic Faith workers have been arrested in Whittier, but it has only increased the interest and deepened the work.

An anointed handkerchief was sent to Elizabeth Smith, Brunswick, Ga., and as soon as she opened the letter, she was instantly healed.

We have heard the funeral of the Gospel preached, the power of nobody unto nothing, now we are preaching the power of God unto salvation.

One came here that had been suffering for years in body, and was healed by the power of God while in the meeting without even asking for prayers.

A young lady was contemplating suicide came to the meeting and was saved, then sanctified and baptized with the Holy Ghost. She is very happy in the Lord.

When the conditions are just right, the Lord is just as responsible for the healing of our body as of our souls. The reason so many are sick, is because they trust in the arm of flesh instead of God.

A brother testified, "Last week I came in a backslider and half drunk and the Lord forgave my backsliding right in my seat, and a few days afterward, He sanctified me and baptized me with the Holy Ghost."

The gift of tongues is the glory of God flooding your soul and the Spirit taking possession. You will never know what it means to be clay in the hands of the Potter until you receive the Pentecostal baptism.

Pentecost has fallen in Long Beach, Cal. Souls are slain under the power of God and meetings cannot close. A number have received the baptism with the Holy Ghost. The Lord is using Bro. E. McCauley to push the work there.

It was God's eternal purpose that Jesus should be born in a humble place. No place is too humble for Jesus to dwell in. He poured out His Spirit in the humblest meeting place in Los Angeles, that no flesh should glory in His presence.

Interpreted message spoken in tongues: "Open your heart and receive the Spirit. I will give good gifts to My children. Blessed are they that trust in me. O drink of the living waters. Believe in Me. O believe in Me, and ye shall find everything ye ask for."

The meeting has been a melting time. The people are all melted together by the power of the blood and the Holy Ghost. They are made one lump, one bread, all one body in Christ Jesus. There is no Jew or Gentile, bond or free, in the Azusa Street Mission.

Bro. A. Sulger, a Danish young man from Chicago, has received his Pentecost and is filled and saturated with the melting power of God. He expects to be on his way east soon, and, as the Lord opens the way, will go to Denmark where the Lord is calling him to preach the Gospel. His father is a Lutheran preacher.

Bro. Tom Hezmalhalch has returned for a short time to Los Angeles from Chicago, Colorado Springs, Denver, and other places where the Lord has been using him and reports a wonderful work of God in those places and that many souls are being saved, healed, and baptized with the Holy Ghost, with signs following.

"Jesus is coming again soon. Do not reject His voice. Don't reject Him, don't reject Him. He was nailed on the cross for you." The above is the interpretation of a message in unknown language given by one who came a sinner and is now filled with the Holy Ghost speaking and preaching in new tongues.

A brother writes that he received the baptism with the Holy Ghost on a Santa Fe train running forty miles an hour, and ten more after him received the same gift. They were all waiting for the promise of the Father. He is no respecter of persons or places. To tarry at Jerusalem is to wait at Jesus' feet wherever you are in His will.

Companies of Christians in many places are waiting on God, tarrying for the baptism with the Holy Ghost. The most spiritual people in this land and across the ocean, and missionaries in foreign lands are writing that they are seeking the Pentecost. This is a significant fact. It means that the Lord is preparing His people for His soon coming.

On Thanksgiving day a baptismal service was held at the Pentecostal Mission on Maple and Eighth Streets, where there is a baptistry. Twenty-four were baptized by immersion. The Spirit of God was upon the people. The candidates for baptism were filled with the Spirit and shouted and praised God as they came out of the water.

Sister Hagg is now back in Los Angeles from Ft. Worth, Tex., rejoicing in the Holy Ghost and continually witnessing to the Pentecost, which she received last May. She says,

"Now a single doubt about this blessing of God. I know I was sanctified before, and I know this is separate from sanctification. He fills me with His glory. Since I have received the baptism with the Holy Ghost, I have understood God better and His truth has opened up to me as never before. It enables me to stand in every place. I have sweet fellowship with my Lord in all trials and tests. The Lord gave me the interpretation of some words I was speaking in the unknown tongue and the interpretation was, 'My soul cannot tell it.'"

FROM LOS ANGELES TO HOME AND FOREIGN FIELDS

Workers are constantly going out trusting God alone for their support. A Band of six missionaries left for Africa. They are Bro. and Sister S. J. Mead, Bro. and Sister Robert Shideler, and Bro. and Sister G. W. Batman. Address them at Longs Temperance Hotel, Liverpool, England, Lime St. They are going to two points in Africa. God bless them and make them a great blessing.

We must keep them on our hearts in prayer for they are our brothers and sisters.

Some who have left for home fields are H. M. Turney for San Jose; J. G. Wilkin, for points north; Bro. G. Zigler, Swanton, Ohio; F. E. Hill, J. C. Mackey, Bro. and Sister Lopez for San Diego; Ivy Campbell, T. W. Sargent, and Bro. and Sister W. H. Miller for points in Ohio; and Bro. and Sister Eric Hollingsworth en route to Sweden. The Lord is sending revivals everywhere that workers have gone that are baptized with the Holy Ghost and fire. Many more are being fitted up and called for the field, for the fields are white ready for the harvest.

EN ROUTE TO AFRICA

Bro. and Sister G. W. Batman who last wrote from New York on their way to Monrovia, Liberia, Africa, are tried and true workers and have the enduement of power from on high and the fitness of the gift of tongues. Their faith was severely tested as to their fare. A brother who paid the most of their fare was praying the night before they left that the Lord would give him some revelation. So that night the Lord showed him a lamb that was tied and told him to loose it and as he did so, a great Shekina glory shone in the room. The Lord showed him later that it meant the missionaries he was to be the means of sending on their way. They started with faith in God though they were taking their three little children and their destination is called the "white man's graveyard." They did not have more than their fare to New York. They have the gift of healing and we believe God will wonderfully use them among those darkened souls.

BRO. G. W. BATMAN'S TESTIMONY

I was converted nine years ago, and got a know-so salvation—no guess work about it. I repented of my sins and forsook them, accepting the Lord as my Savior. Praise God. A few years later, I fasted and prayed for about three days and during that time I put off the old man Adam in the form of inbred sin and God came in and destroyed the devil's workshop by casting his tools on the outside. Praise God I got a real evidence that I was sanctified and the Blood applied. After that, I received the baptism with the Holy Ghost and fire and now I feel the presence of the Holy Ghost, not only in my heart but in my lungs, my hands, my arms and all through my body and at times I am shaken like a locomotive steamed up and prepared for a long journey. O it is blessed to let the Lord have His way with you. I also speak in six foreign tongues given me at God's command. God has called me to Africa as a missionary, and told me to go to Monrovia, Liberia. He showed me the town which is on the west coast. I described the town and country to Bro. Mead, a missionary that had been there and he said it was a perfect description. Saints, pray much. Fast and pray.

MRS. DAISY BATMAN'S TESTIMONY

At the age of fourteen the Lord saved me from my sin. Last April He sanctified my soul, took all inbred sin out and gave me a clean heart fit for the Lord's use. Hallelujah! But still I hungered for more, so when the Pentecost came to Los Angeles, I found that was just what I wanted. But I was working every day and could not be at the meeting much. One day the Lord told me to stop everything and go to the meeting. I said, Lord, I have three small children and no way to support them. He said, I will supply your needs. Glory to God, He has supplied all our needs. We have never needed for anything and have never asked anybody but the blessed Lord for a penny. Three years ago last April, the Lord gave us the call to Africa. At first I thought I would stay and let my husband go, but He said, "No, you must go too." I thought He wanted us to go right away, but when He saw I was willing to spend my life in Africa for precious souls, He revealed to us that He would tell us when to go. And three months after we received our baptism, He said, "Now go to Africa." O glory to God, I am so glad I got to the place where the blessed Lord's will is my will."

BAPTIZED IN MINNEAPOLIS

Bro. Otto Braulin of 2112 Fourth Ave., Minneapolis, Minn., writes that he has received his Pentecost through reading the paper and personal correspondence. He speaks in two unknown tongues. He says, "I laid the paper to one side, went aside into a room and asked God if I was really and truly cleansed by the Word, and I got the mighty answer of God through my whole being that I was. Am I cleansed by the blood? I got the same mighty powerful witness. Then I said to my Father, I have not the baptism with the Holy Ghost, because I have not the gift of tongues, the evidence of Pentecost, and the power began to work as peculiarly and forcibly as never before. That very night I got the evidence, as the Holy Ghost gave utterance in two unknown tongues. I could distinguish the difference between the two. Since then the power becomes stronger and the Spirit speaks plainer and more mightily. The power of God streams through my whole body. (I suppose the healing power.) I have fallen on the floor through the mighty power coming upon me. I was in a mission last Sunday and in the afternoon the Spirit came on me and the Spirit fell on the clean souls. They said showers of power came upon them and they were set free. In the evening the leaders set themselves against the speaking in tongues because I cannot interpret, but the power was so mighty upon me they could see it was not man's but God's."

JAPANESE HEAR IN THEIR OWN TONGUE

Pueblo, Colorado, is a city of many nationalities. In the steel works alone that employs 500 men, seventeen languages are spoken. There are Greeks, Chinese, Japanese and many others. There is a wonderful field. The Lord had opened up a mission there when the Pentecostal Gospel came. The woman in charge of the mission went right to seeking and received the baptism and before she got off her knees, was speaking in Chinese. One day when she was speaking, the Spirit began to speak another language through her. Nobody understand till they saw some uneasiness manifested in the back of the room where some Japanese were sitting. They began to wring their hands and cry and bury their face in their hands. Someone went to them and they said, "Talk my tongue. Tell me all about my God how He died for the Japanese." They had never heard anything like that before.

REVIVAL IN INDIA
WONDERFUL POURING OUT OF GOD'S SPIRIT AMONG THE NATIVES OF THE KHASSIA HILLS

The great revival still continues, and wonderful manifestations of the power of God are surely among these nations. An article in the "Herald of Light" says: "It was a grand and inspiring sight to see these people marching in parties to the Assembly, and along the way would halt and have prayer and praise meetings, and their conversations were continually about the wonderful works of God. The assembly is held in a small village called Malrang, and many thousands of people have come up to this assembly, and God has shown himself in power and blessings. Many other portions of India are being awakened by true spirit. The glorious and awful scenes portrayed are only the fulfillment of prophecy, and doubtless the outgrowth of years of toil and prayers.

In another station in India, in a service in a mission, about two hundred were under conviction for sin, and crying for mercy, and the meeting continued for six hours. A report from another locality says that men, women and children were heard at daybreak singing hymns which the missionaries had been trying for months to teach them. The Holy Ghost was working mightily, and soon there was an outburst of prayer and praise of new-born souls. Men, women and children called on the Lord day and night, and there was no cessation of the meetings."

Those who receive the baptism with the Holy Ghost and speak in tongues and backslide from this state may retain the speaking in tongues for a while after divine love is gone, but gradually this gift also will melt away. A very little harshness or a critical suspicious statement about a brother will grieve the tender, sensitive Spirit. A careful and constant guard must be made, lest the flesh arise and destroy the walk. Preachers often go too far and try to emphasize in fleshly vehemence a good point made by the Spirit. All such conduct will receive a gentle rebuke of the Spirit, and if heartily repented of, will soon be overcome, and result in greater confirmation of God's power in the life.

—"Apostolic Light"

William J. Seymour at the peak of the Azusa Street Revival

Five

Beginning of Worldwide Revival, January 1907

The Apostolic Faith

"Earnestly contend for the faith which was once delivered unto the saints."—Jude 3

Vol. 1, No. 5, Los Angeles, Cal., January, 1907, Subscription Free

We are expecting wonderful things from the Lord for 1907. The closing up of the old year and beginning of the new found us on our knees at Azusa Mission. And as the new year was announced, such a wave of glory, and divine love and unity came over us. The meeting went on till morning and all the next day. It is a jubilee year. May we all spend it at His feet, learning of Him.

The Lord did great things in 1906. Pentecost first fell in Los Angeles on April 9th. Since then the good tidings has spread in two hemispheres. Many are rejoicing in pardon, purity, and the power of the Holy Ghost. Wherever the work goes, souls are saved, and not only saved from hell but through and through, and prepared to meet the Lord at His coming. Hundreds have been baptized with the Holy Ghost. Many of them are now out in the field, and some in foreign lands, and God is working with them, granting signs and wonders to follow the preaching of the full Gospel.

People all over the land have heard that the oil of the Spirit is being poured out in Los Angeles, and they are coming for oil— coming thousands of miles. And they are being filled with the holy oil, the baptism with the Holy Ghost, and wherever they go, it is being poured out.

From the little mustard seed faith that was given to a little company of people waiting on God in a cottage prayer meeting, a great tree has grown, so that people from all parts of the country are coming like birds to lodge in the branches thereof. (Matt. 13:31–32.) The faith is still growing, and we are just in the beginning, earnestly contending for the faith once delivered unto the saints.

It is a continual upper room tarrying at Azusa Street. It is like a continual camp-meeting or convention. All classes and nationalities meet on a common level. One who came for the first time said, "The thing that impressed me most was the humility of the people, and I went to my room and got down on my knees and asked God to give me humility."

The altars are filled with seekers. Sometimes the meetings go on all night. People are slain under the power of God and sanctified or rise up speaking in new tongues. In the meetings, you see the holy joy of the Lord in the countenances, and people are melted in the presence of the Lord, filled with His praises.

The Lord is graciously healing many sick bodies. People are healed at the Mission almost every day. Requests come in for prayer from all over. They are presented in the meeting and the Spirit

witnesses in many cases that prayer is answered, and when we hear from them they are healed. Handkerchiefs are sent in to be blest, and are returned to the sick and they are healed in many cases. One day nine handkerchiefs were blest, another day sixteen. A man came with a broken arm and was healed. The mission people never take medicine. They do not want it. They have taken Jesus for their healer and He always heals.

There is a very sweet spirit of unity among Pentecostal missions in Los Angeles and workers in suburban towns. Every Monday morning, the misiners and workers from these different points meet together for prayer and counsel. The missions in Los Angeles are at 327½ S. Spring, of which Bro. Fisher is the pastor; 8th and Maple Ave., of which Bro. Pendleton is the pastor; and 1321 E. 51st St., where Bro. and Sister Kent have charge. Workers from Long Beach, Pasadena, Clearwater, Anaheim, and other nearby places also come in. All are in one accord. In our first meeting several messages were given in tongues through our Bro. Post, and interpreted as follows:

We acknowledge Christ only, His truth, His Word. We must acknowledge that He is in our midst, walking among the golden candlesticks, pruning, purging. He who moved among the golden candlesticks, is moving in our midst now. We must recognize Him along as Head over all, and know no man after the flesh. The Spirit of God will teach us, if we keep low in love and humility before Him. Our Lord says, "I smile upon you, when you are seeking My will, My glory only. There must be no glorying in names or orders of systems, only in Myself alone. All fullness is in me, all power is in My Gospel."

We must give God all the glory in this work. We must keep very humble at His feet. He recognizes no flesh, no color, no names. We must not glory in Azusa Mission, nor in anything but the Lord Jesus Christ by whom the world is crucified unto us and we unto the world.

We stand as assemblies and missions all in perfect harmony. Azusa Mission stands for the unity of God's people everywhere. God is uniting His people, baptizing them by one Spirit into one body.

PENTECOST RESTORED

Written after his Pentecostal anointing on the train by J. W. Ellison, Des Moines, Iowa.

O glorious promise of
    heaven!
Fulfilled to His people at
    last;
The tongues of fire have
    descended,
And sealed us as those in
    the past.

The Pentecost power is
    now spreading,
The Bible rings clear as a
    bell.
The finished work of the
    Saviour,
We now are commissioned
    to tell.

The touch of the hand
    brings conviction.
The look of the eye startles
    sin.
The flood gates of heaven

are opened,
And souls are now enter-
ing in.

All fear is banished forever,
And sickness and pain flee
away,
The touch of Jesus is as
powerful
As it was in that wonder-
ful day.

The union of hearts is like
magic,
And bodies are molded
like clay;
Souls that are sealed by
His Spirit
Have entered the heaven-
lies to stay.

Sinners who once have
been careless
Have wakened to a sense
of their need;
Pentecost surely is spreading,
Regardless of doctrine or
creed.

Then glory to Jesus who
loved me,
And glory to Jesus who
came,
And glory to Jesus who
fills me,
And seals with His own
precious name.

PENTECOSTAL POWER IN SAN DIEGO
San Diego, Cal.,
Jan. 5.

Dear Saints, Greeting!

Grace and peace be multi-
plied unto you all, through
our Lord Jesus Christ, who
always causeth us to triumph
in every place, and maketh
manifest through us the savor
of His knowledge.

The dear Lord has favored
us with continuous victory,
reclaimed, sanctified, and
some baptized with the Holy
Ghost every week. The interest
is increasing, notwithstanding
the continuous wet weather.
The altar is filled with seekers
at most every service.

We have had some marvel-
ous cases where those possessed
by the devil have been wonderfully and completely delivered and clothed in their right
minds. We wish to note one
case in particular for the glory
of God and the power of our
Lord Jesus Christ.

A man of German birth
came in the meetings, a
master of Theosophy and Spiritualism, who claimed he was

Christ incarnate—that he was immortal, and had all wisdom and knowledge. The blessed Holy Ghost gave the saints the discerning of Spirits, and they rebuked the devils in him. And the man fell to the floor, trembling from head to foot. The devils were commanded to come out of him in Jesus' name. And immediately he began to confess his sins and crimes, too awful to mention. He continued to pray and call upon God for mercy, and in a few days he found peace. He has since gone on to the cleansing Blood, and has received his Pentecost, and in humility is owning Jesus as his perfect Savior, clothed in his right mind, joyful and happy.

About twelve have received their Pentecost and a number are still seeking. We are praying that the Lord will establish this work as in Los Angeles. This is an open field with virgin soil, and the work is taking deep and firm hold upon the people. Our hearts are burdened for salvation of the people of San Diego. —F. E. Hill

AKRON VISITED WITH PENTECOST
113 Oak St., Akron, Ohio, Dec. 27th

Since I first heard of the wonderful way God was working in Los Angeles, my heart got hungry. And the dear saints in Akron kept up a steady cry to God day and night for Him to send it this way. And before we hardly knew it, Akron was visited. Glory to God! He sent dear Ivy Campbell here in answer to prayer, and many have received their Pentecost. The altar is more than filled nearly every service. In fact there is hardly a break in the meeting. Some people bring lunches and don't stop to eat them. Some of the sisters sing in tongues like voices from heaven and also interpret some. O, it is wonderful! Many demons have been cast out and the sick are being healed. Glory to Jesus! He is also selecting His missionaries. The meeting runs day and night—sometimes all night.

People come from miles around here and are receiving their personal Pentecost.

Bro. McKinney is sending out invitations far and near, and telling how God is visiting Akron, and it brings in the hungry ones. His church doors were opened wide to welcome dear Sisters Ivy Campbell and Hudson from East Liverpool. The meetings have been running over three weeks. The Holy Ghost is the only leader. Praise God!

While some of the prominent ministers are opposing it, yet their hungry members jump over the fence and get to the little mission church and get saved, sanctified, and then receive their personal Pentecost. We are glad God had one humble preacher in Akron who opened wide the door to receive this "latter rain." We are likely just getting the first sprinkling of the great shower that is to come. Praise God!

The burden of everyone that has received their personal Pentecost is, "Jesus is coming soon."

Jan. 21.—The fire has broken out in Pittsburgh too. God is visiting every hungry town and city that will receive Him.

The fire is spreading here, in spite of all the water the devil pours on. It seems to act like oil instead of water. Glory to our conquering King!

One of our mothers in Israel has her personal Pentecost and the Hawaiian language. Three Hawaiian boys from Honolulu came to Akron to get work, and God sent them to the Mission, and they said Mother Davis had the Hawaiian language perfectly and interpreted two messages she gave out, which were, "God is love," and "Jesus is coming soon."—Yours in Jesus, Mrs. Pearl Bowen

PORTLAND IS STIRRED
Portland, Ore., Dec. 31st
Peace from God the Father be unto you and all the saints.

Well, God has stirred up this North till every devil in hell is stirred also.

I finished my work in Salem: was there two weeks. Seven received Pentecost. The saints are in perfect harmony. Students, city officials and the first people of the place heard the Gospel, but as far as we can see now, they have rejected the

Gospel. Most of the ones that received their Pentecost are from the little places around, and they have gone home to spread the glad tidings of this precious Gospel. O my heart is so full this morning. Glory! Glory! Glory!

Well, Sister Glassco and three of her children got their Pentecost in Salem. And before they got home, on Christmas day, while Bro. Glassco was preaching, Pentecost fell on the meeting and two spoke with tongues. We had planned to come on Saturday and this was Tuesday. When we got here, three more had received the baptism. We arrived here at noon and went into the meeting at three. The power fell before the meeting was half through and two received Pentecost; at night, two more. Last night Mildred received her Pentecost. The slain of the Lord lay so you can't move about the altar. The altar is full before the meeting is half over. The house is just packed. O if we only had a larger hall. I cannot tell how God is working here.

Now I must tell you about Mildred. She spoke in four tongues and sang so sweetly and interpreted every word. The interpretation of the song was:

"Jesus is calling you.

Jesus is calling, O sinner, come home.

Glory to His name, O sinner, come home."

Then she arose and the crowd was silenced like death. She began to wave her arms and preach in tongues and interpret. Will give you a part of it. "He that comes unto me, I will in no wise cast out." (Tongues.) "The Lord has prepared me to preach His Gospel." (Tongues.) "Jesus is coming soon." (Tongues.) "He will take away His bride, one will be taken and the other left."

Jan. 8.—The crowds throng the hall. We have to have a policeman to keep the aisles clear. They tell us throngs of people come and are turned away. The Zion people held a mass meeting Sunday and decided to come in a body for their Pentecost.

O I am so glad that He has chosen me. The Lord has healed some bad cases. One woman had epileptic fits. When the devil went out of her, she was so weak she could not stand. A man's hand that was helpless was healed. A woman with her mind almost gone was healed in the hall last night before the sinners' eyes.

Pentecost falls on people when they come the second time to the meeting, sitting in their seats.

I stay in the mission. It's humble quarters, but Jesus is here. Every minute of my time is given to God. I get tired sometimes. Was sent to pray for a man with a high fever. I prayed before I went, was so tired. Jesus said, "I do the healing." When I got there, Jesus healed him before I laid hands on him. He got up and came to meeting. Oh, I am learning the wondrous secret: It is letting Jesus do the work and carry all the load. Oh, I am so happy in His love and service.

People from all over are coming. A young lady came from Albany. She was a sinner and got all, even to her Pentecost, yesterday, in one day. There are 38 now that have received the baptism, eight since Saturday, and this is Tuesday morning.

I hear the work in San Francisco is fine. Souls saved, sanctified and baptized, and the church people coming in. Oh, God is spreading this Gospel in spite of the devil. How glad I am I ever found my way into the dear old mission on Azusa St. Love to all the saints. —Florence Crawford, 215 2nd Ave.

APOSTOLIC FAITH MISSION IN SAN JOSE
San Jose, Cal., Jan. 24.

Dear Apostolic Faith:

God our Father has been doing great things for us since we last wrote. We are now worshiping in our own hall. We have a very nicely furnished mission, for which we praise the Lord.

The fire is still falling. Last Sunday we had a wonderful all-day meeting. The slaying power was manifest in a remarkable manner. One lay for hours under the power. A young girl took God at His Word, opened her mouth wide, and the Lord filled it with praises in new tongues.

A Mrs. Williamson brought her daughter to the meetings for healing for her eyes, which were very bad. The power was present to heal and the child went home completely recovered. Many others have been healed since the meeting opened. Sister Williamson has received her Pentecost and God has put her in His heavenly choir, to sing the heavenly songs for His glory. She also writes in many languages. She interprets most of the songs that she sings, and when she speaks in tongues, she also interprets.

Several of those who have received their Pentecost have been called to the foreign field to labor for Him. One young woman is making preparations to leave for Hawaii very soon.

I am just holding the fort till my Father sends someone to take charge of the work here, when I expect to leave

for a trip around the world, sounding the golden trumpet, heralding the year of jubilee. For the coming of the Lord is near, even at the door. And he wants the heathen nations to hear the glad tidings and be ready for His coming.

I believe this movement is the last call that the world will receive before He comes for His bride. Rev. 19:7, 8. These are the days of preparation. Nahum 2:1–5. The chariots that Nahum saw are the automobiles which we see running in our streets today.

I am anxious to be on the go, for I feel that the time is short. What we do, we must do while it is day.

—H. M. Turney

PENTECOST IN NORTH CAROLINA
Dunn, N. C., Jan. 2.

To the Saints in Azusa Mission, through all California, greetings in Jesus Name!

O praise Him! It is wonderful. Last week I held a few services in the country in one of the Holiness churches, and two received their Pentecost and spoke in tongues. The languages were as perfect as I ever heard. One was a Sunday school superintendent and the other an elder of the church. I had to leave that meeting to fill my appointment here, but the meeting is still going on there.

This is only the third day and already about ten have received their Pentecost. Five preachers received the baptism and some of them have two or three languages already and can preach sermons and pray in the tongues. The church is filled to overflow and people come from all over the country. Sinners are being converted and others repenting. This town of about 2,500 has never seen Pentecost before, but praise God, it has come and the town is stirred from center to circumference. People have laid aside eating and business to a great extent and are going down before God in earnest. How I praise God for this wonderful salvation. All the signs follow me since I received Pentecost. O let us trust only to the still,

sweet voice of Jesus. He does it all. O how I praise God for sending me to Los Angeles, and for you all.

Jan. 17.—Our God is fulfilling His promise and His Spirit is being poured out here in Dunn as never before. Many have come from South Carolina and Georgia and have received their Pentecost and gone back, and fire is spreading. The meeting continues here in greater interest. Nearly every service, someone receives their Pentecost and speaks in tongues. Some of our preachers have preached, sung and prayed in unknown tongues, and without speaking a word of English, have awakened sinners.

Several colored people have received their Pentecost and speak in tongues. God has wonderfully blest some of the people with the gift of song. One colored sister, a school teacher, received the Pentecost the other night and spoke in tongues for some time. She has manifested a call to foreign fields. All the people of God are one here.

I prayed much that God would give me access to my brethren, and this I might convince them of His blessed truths. And not one of them has taken issue against me as yet, but come forward and have received their real Pentecost and are going forth in the power of the Lord. Some of the people are getting ready for the foreign fields now. O how I praise God!

Brothers, pray, and spread the tidings around wherever man is found. I may never see you in the flesh any more, but I am coming in bringing in the sheaves.

Many are getting their Pentecost at home and abroad. I go from here to High Point, N. C. Have more calls than I can fill in six months.

Your brother and servant of God.—G. B. Cashwell

PENTECOST IN LAMONT, OKLA.

Jan. 17th.

Dear Saints, Greetings!

Left Los Angeles Dec. 4, and arrived in Oklahoma just one week later, making a few stops on the way. Quite a number were tarrying and waiting for Pentecost when I arrived, but much had to be done before God could pour out His Spirit. The people had been in much bondage. Eating pork, wearing neckties, drinking coffee, and wearing a moustache were taught to be very sinful, and except you were circumcised to these you were lost.

After about ten days of prayer and holding up the Blood, God began to break them up and they began to beg pardon of one another and their neighbors. And in a short time, in a cottage prayer meeting, God poured out His Spirit in slaying power and nearly all went down, one woman coming through speaking in tongues. God now began to work and souls were saved, backsliders reclaimed, and believers sanctified at nearly every service. The country was stirred for miles around. Some came 100 miles to get Pentecost and healing.

One lady who had been a Free Methodist was reclaimed and sanctified and baptized with the Holy Ghost. She speaks and sings in tongues, and her husband got under such conviction he could scarcely do His work, and in a few days came to the altar and was beautifully saved. 'Tis so sweet to trust in Jesus.

The Lord told me to move on, last Sunday. Meeting closed Sunday night with many seekers at the altar. The saints will go right on and push the battle.

Jan. 21.—Arrived here Friday morning after spending two days in Chicago. Quite a number here are seeking the baptism. We expect great things here. Pray much for me. I can feel it when they pray for me in public. Some time ago in a prayer service, the Lord showed me Bro. Seymour praying for me, and I seemed to be carried away in the Spirit.—Under the Blood, G. A. Cook, 612 Terrace Ave., Indianapolis, Ind.

Several have already received the baptism with the Holy Ghost in Des Moines, Ia. It was not through anyone sent there, but they were tarrying before God and Pentecost fell.

In Toronto, a number have received the baptism. Bro. O. Adams went there from Los Angeles. He had not yet received his Pentecost, but told them about what God had done in Azusa Mission and other places. They went right to tarrying before God. A company stayed after meeting to pray through and the Spirit fell and three were filled with the Holy Ghost.

We are receiving hundreds of names and addresses for the paper. Please write very plainly. Those who ask for it regularly are enrolled on the books. We are sending out thousands of sample copies to friends whose names are sent in by others. If we do not hear from these, we sent only two of three numbers. Please notify us of any mistakes.

If you want to keep fat and filled with the power of the

Holy Ghost, live off of the Word.

The Lord is enabling us to publish another issue of 30,000 papers for the fifth number of the Apostolic Faith. He has greatly blest in getting it out. Though it is somewhat late, we trust it will be the greater blessing.

When you were poor and ugly in your own sight, then was the time God exalted and used you, but when you get to be some great Nebuchadnezzar, then God turns you out to eat the grass like an ox. Keep little and God will use you.

A baby that accidentally took poison that it found in a bottle in a closet, was healed in answer to prayer. The mother held on to God in agonizing prayer, "Lord, save my baby." The little thing was cold, but the Lord healed it completely.

"The Holy Ghost is blessing us daily, but we must have a great outpouring of the Holy Spirit, for there are people in our midst that are praying night and day for a great awakening among the people." —Mrs. C. A. Roll, 1005 Edwards St., Fort Worth, Tex., Jan. 9.

Sickness is the work of Satan. Sometimes we bring it upon ourselves by overexertion. Sometimes it is permitted of the Lord because of sins of omission or commission. Satan cannot afflict us unless God permits. He has no power over us unless we get on his territory.

Souls are getting the baptism in Clearwater, Cal. Mother Wheaton went down to tarry with them and was baptized with the Holy Ghost and spoke in two languages. She is very happy and filled with the Holy Ghost and God is using her. Bro. McLain writes that there are lots of hungry souls there and the devil is stirred.

Several have written and asked if we received the offerings sent. We can answer that they all came safely, even to some letters that came through the fire in a train wreck and were scorched on the edges and stained by water, but they came safely and money in them. So we see how the Lord takes care of consecrated offerings.

"I received my Pentecost last Saturday morning, 1.15 a.m. Praise God! I am wholly given up to His will. Words cannot express the blessed peace I have in my soul. My soul is filled with His glory. Hallelujah! Praise God for His wonderful Gift to men. We are praying for and expecting 120 Spirit-baptized souls to take San Diego for God." —H. G., San Diego, Cal.

"The Scandinavian people here are receiving their Pentecost. I was with them in their watch night meeting. O how God poured out His Spirit on all flesh. Many spoke in tongues and sang the songs of heaven—a heavenly choir. Some fell under the power of God. My soul doth magnify the Lord. He thrills my spirit, soul and body." —Mrs. S. C. Magle, 710 Times St., Ballard, Wash.

A sanctified body is one in perfect health, through faith in God. It does not mean we could not get sick, but we are maintained in health by faith. We do not want to teach people they cannot get sick, because they would they were infallible creatures. "As the branch cannot bear fruit except it abide in the vine, no more can ye except ye abide in Me." So we must abide in Christ for health.

In Akron, Ohio, a young man went to the Pentecost meetings and got under conviction through the preaching. And went to the pastor of the First Congregational Church and returned to him $10 that he had stolen about fourteen years before, and promised to pay the rest. The pastor was very much surprised, for the man had been under his preaching for years and never got under conviction. He said, "That kind of religion is loaded with good shot. There are no blank cartridges in it."

Bro. Tom Hezmalhalch has been home to Los Angeles on a visit and we have been feasting together on the good things of Father's table. On his way back to Colorado, the Spirit directed him to stop off at the Needles. Taking the train on Tuesday morning to resume his journey, at four o'clock he passed the train he had taken at Los Angeles for Denver, every car laid in the ditch. By some means they had left the rails. If he had not obeyed the Spirit, he would have been in the ditch and precious souls would have suffered. It pays to know the Lord and obey Him.

William J. Seymour in later years

Six

PENTECOST ON BOTH SIDES OF THE OCEAN, FEBRUARY/MARCH 1907

THE APOSTOLIC FAITH

"Earnestly contend for the faith which was once delivered unto the saints."—Jude 3

Vol. 1, No. 6, Los Angeles, Cal., February-March, 1907, Subscription Free

God is still manifesting His power in Los Angeles.

The Pentecost has crossed the water on both sides to the Hawaiian Islands on the west, and England, Norway, Sweden, and India on the east.

A brother in Honolulu received the Pentecost, by hearing of God's work through the paper. He said when he got down to seeking in earnest, the Lord baptized him with the Holy Ghost and he spoke in two languages.

We rejoice to hear that Pentecost has fallen in Calcutta, India, over ten thousand miles away on the other side of the world. Praise God. We have letters from China, Germany, Switzerland, Norway, Sweden, England, Ireland, Australia and other countries from hungry souls that want their Pentecost. Some of these letters are in foreign languages. Missionaries write that they are hungry for this outpouring of the Spirit which they believe to be the real Pentecost. The world seems ripe for the Pentecost in all lands and God is sending it. Amen.

One of the missionaries from Los Angeles in Liberia, Africa, had been able to speak to the people in the Cru tongue. Another sister there wrote in an unknown language under the power of the Spirit, and it was understood and read by one of the native kings there.

Requests for prayer from hungry souls are coming in from all over.

They want salvation from sin, and sanctification, and the baptism with the Holy Ghost, and healing of their bodies. So the requests are presented and handkerchiefs are blest and the power comes upon us in praying for them; and we receive letters saying that they are receiving their Pentecost and being healed. Praise God.

March 19th was a wonderful day at the Mission on Azusa St. Three ministers from Tennessee received the enduement of power from on high and the glory of God filled the upper room. Others received the anointing of the Spirit and some were slain under the power of God.

Bro. Stewart from Phoenix, Arizona, came to Azusa Mission and sought the baptism with the Holy Ghost, and God laid him out under the power of the Spirit and took complete control of him, speaking through him in tongues. He was filled and overflowing with the Holy Ghost when he returned to Arizona. And Mother Griffith, also from Phoenix, has come and received her baptism.

The work at Azusa Mission is growing deeper and more powerful than ever. Praise God. Meetings continue every day with seekers at every service and the three meetings run very near together. All day meetings on Sunday. Three other Apostolic Faith Missions continue in the city and God's blessing is upon them. The workers from these missions and from suburban towns meet together for conference on Mondays to study the Scriptures and get deeper into the things of God and for conference in the work of the Lord. The spirit of unity, love and power is manifest. Other like missions are being established in a number of towns.

Bro. Andrews and wife, Gospel workers from Tennessee, came to Azusa Mission for the express purpose of receiving their Pentecost and Bro.

Andrews has been baptized with the Holy Ghost and is filled and overflowing with the Spirit. He and his wife were so hungry and had such faith that the Lord wanted them to come, that, not having the means, they started and walked quite a distance, till the Lord gave them the fare, and He is abundantly rewarding them.

Bro. W. H. Durham of 943 North Ave., Chicago, Ill., and Bro. H. L. Blake of Ruthton, Minn., who are both preachers of the Gospel, came to Los Angeles to see and investigate what God was doing. They both were baptized with the Holy Ghost and went back filled and saturated with the power of God, speaking in tongues and magnifying God. It was a great blessing to us to have them with us and see what great things the Lord did for them and the blessing overflowed upon all God's children. They are members of the World's Faith Missionary Association.

Sister Rees from Oakland visited Azusa Mission recently. She brought a report from the saints in Oakland that a leader was needed there in the work, one called and prepared of the Lord. We prayed for God to send someone. Bro. Irwin received the call and went with his wife. His report comes just as the paper is going to press: Oakland, Cal., Mar. 21.—"God is undertaking for us here. Two received their Pentecost last night with Bible evidence. Others are seeking pardon, sanctification, the promise of the Father." —B. H. Irwin.

A number from Winnipeg, Canada, have come to Los Angeles and are now rejoicing in the baptism with the Holy Ghost. Others have come from the Atlantic coast and from Colorado and different states and they have received a Bible Pentecost, evidenced by speaking in tongues, and from other centers workers are going out to the ends of the earth, till we cannot keep track of them.

The Lord is speedily preparing His people for His coming.

We cannot give a report of all that have gone out into the work since the last paper, for they are going almost every day. Bro. and Sister H. McLain have gone to San Jose, Cal., to take charge of the work there and Sister Agnes Jacobson and Bro. Harmon Clifford are also in the work in San Jose. See report from there of how God is working. Bro. Turney and wife who were at San Jose are now in Honolulu. Bro. and Sister E. W. Vinton from near Boston, Mass., who received their Pentecost in Los Angeles, have returned to tell the glad tidings. Their address is 12 Leyden St., Medford, Mass. Bro. C. E. Marah expects to join them there in preaching this Gospel. Bands of workers have gone out to other places and started the work.

Since the last paper, Bro. Seymour visited San Francisco and San Jose and reported that God had some of the most precious saints there filled with the Holy Ghost and shining for God that he had ever seen and that the power of God was wonderfully manifest.

There are a number of papers on the Apostolic line that are springing up. We cannot tell how many there are, because we hear of new ones we have not seen. But there are three clean cut papers besides Apostolic Faith, out and out for a Bible Pentecost according to Acts. 2: 4 and with subscription free. They are the "Apostolic Light," Portland Ore., "The New Acts," Alliance, Ohio (which now includes "Pentecostal Wonders") and "The Apostolic Evangel," Royston, Ga. (formerly "Live Coals.") These papers are all about the size of the January number of this paper and they are filled with the wonderful works of God, and are spreading the glad tidings of another Pentecost all over the world. They are all supported entirely by freewill offerings.

PENTECOST IN OTHER LANDS

IN LONDON

23 Gairloch Road, Camberwell, S. E., London, Jan. 20.— A little band of Christians have been waiting here about nine months for their Pentecost and am glad to say one sister has received her Pentecost with tongues. Praise Him! Will you continue to pray that all may receive, the writer included. I feel very hungry.—Yours in Jesus Christ, C. H. Hook

IN STOCKHOLM

Stockholm, Sweden, March 8.—Please, dear ones, help us to praise the Lord. The first soul came through tonight receiving the baptism with the Holy Ghost and Bible evidence. Bless God! —Eric Hollingsworth and wife

This message was just received from our brother and sister who have gone to Sweden with this precious Gospel. They wrote of the salvation and sanctification of souls and now we rejoice with them that Pentecost has fallen in Sweden's capitol.

IN SWEDEN

We are having a wonderful time in Sweden. Hundreds have been saved and sanctified. Over a hundred baptized with the Holy Ghost. Praise God! Glory! Glory! Glory! Many have been healed by the dear Lord. Signs as on the day of Pentecost are following, talking and singing in tongues. I cannot tell you all now that God has been doing. The work is spreading fast. Many are seeking for a clean heart and there is oneness among God's people. God shall have all the glory.

I am still talking and writing in tongues. A missionary interpreted what I have been writing in Syriac and Armenian. I was singing Chinese one night, a missionary said. I am busy every day and going from place to place. Strong opposition from many, but God gives the victory. Glory! —Andrew G. Johnson, 48 Skofde, Sweden

IN HONOLULU

Honolulu, Hawaii, March 11.—Immediately upon our arrival here, we found two wholly consecrated souls, hungering for more of God. Bro. Mayfield threw his mission open to us and told us to go to work. So we opened fire upon the enemy the first night of our arrival here. God owned and blest the truth. Nine have received their Pentecost, and in every case they have spoken in new tongues. Sister Mayfield has received her Pentecost and healing for lung trouble. Myself and wife have both spoken in the Korean language, Koreans present testifying to the same. We believe that will be our next field of labor. —H. M. Turney and wife

IN CALCUTTA, INDIA

Feb. 21.—The Lord has led Sister Nelson and myself here to Calcutta to behold the wonderful works of God. He has sent three of His witnesses from America, filled with the Holy Ghost, to show forth His power and proclaim this wonderful Gospel which we and many others have been hungering for so long. Praise His dear name! It is Mr. and Mrs. A. G. Garr and Miss Gammon. God is working in mighty power in our midst. Several have received the baptism with the Holy Ghost and speak with tongues, and many have been saved. We have meetings every day beginning about four p. m. and go on as long as the Lord leads. We are so hungry and do believe that God will soon satisfy our longing souls. —Mary Johnson, Dehiwai, Court Lodge, Ceylon, India

IN NORWAY

Solfies, Pl. 2, Christiania, Norway, Jan. 29.—God is wonderfully demonstrating His power here in the Norwegian capital. It is about ten days since I held the first meeting in the large gymnasium that will take when crowded from 1,500 to 2,000 people. People from all denominations are rushing to the meetings. Over twenty have received their Pentecost and are speaking in tongues. Several have been in trances and had heavenly visions. Some have seen Jesus at our meetings, and the tongues of fire have been seen again over my heard by a freethinker, convincing him of the power of God. Many are seeking salvation and souls are being gloriously saved. Hundreds are seeking a clean heart, and the fire is falling on the purified sacrifice. The fire is spreading very rapidly. Glory to God! I received word from the country districts that the fire is falling there. People who have attended the meetings are taking the fire with them to the towns around about. The account of God's work for my soul has been inserted in many religious papers, and has caused a stir. All can see it is the work of God's Holy Spirit. Hallelujah! Some of the languages spoken are European. One man was thrown on his back, a preacher, last Sunday morning in the Students' Hall, and when he rose, he spoke in four languages, one of these was English. He could speak none of them before. After that, he prophesied and invited sinners to come to Christ. Numbers threw themselves down and cried for salvation, cleansing, and the fiery baptism with the Spirit. Praised be God! Several preachers are seeking their Pentecost. Go on praying for the advancement of the Kingdom of our Lord and Kin in this grand old country. Fraternal greetings from those baptized with the power and fire from on high.—Yours in Christ Jesus, T. B. Barratt

-----

If you get the light on your soul, you will go forward or else backslide.

The more of the Holy Ghost you have, the more love, the more humility, the more praises.

This is not a "do, do" religion, but it is the religion of the Lord Jesus Christ. Man has got to be born again. You cannot get it through moral culture, refinement, or giving up, but you must be born into it. It is through God's beloved Son who washes you, cleanses you, and makes you a fit subject for heaven.

Every sanctified person has the abiding anointing in their soul, and they know His Blood cleanses every moment, but you need the baptism with the Holy Ghost which is the enduement of power, that will make you a witness to the uttermost parts of the earth.

This Gospel cost us too much to run off into fanaticism and be led by visions and dreams. When we get spiritual, there is greater temptation to get puffed up. We must put all visions and dreams on the square of God's Word and try them. The Word must prove all things. When we throw down God's truth, the plummet of His Word, it shows up the counterfeit.

People receive the baptism with the Holy Ghost while about their work. One sister in Whittier received hers while she was baking a cake.

The Holy Ghost is a real living Person that comes down upon you in great and mighty power. Dear loved ones, when He comes upon you, you know it. When He comes in, He comes talking. Your jaws will be unloosed, and He will commence speaking through you.

We are Christ's spiritual bride now, but there is to be a real wedding take place and a real marriage supper. Those that sit down to this supper will be His queen, the ones that have made their robes white and have the seal of God in their foreheads. O let us not miss this supper. We are listening now for the sound of His chariot wheels.

The Lord has taken Spiritualism and Christian Science out of people in this mission, and filled them with the Spirit, and they are sitting at the feet of Jesus. We teach against Theosophy, Christian Science, Magnetic Healing, Spiritualism, Hypnotism and all works of the devil.

NEW SCANDINAVIAN
REVIVAL
THE WITNESS OF
"TONGUES" MANIFESTED
IN CHRISTIANIA

The following report of the Pentecostal revival in Norway is published in the North Mail, Edinburg, England. It is a letter from the Vicar of All Saints, Sunderland, England, Bro. A. A. Body. He had been to Christiania, Norway, visiting Bro. Barratt's meeting.

My four days in Christiania cannot easily be forgotten. I remember well the scenes two years ago, when I stood with Evan Roberts in the pulpit at Ton-y-Pandy, but, wonderful as such scenes in Wales were, the scenes in the Torvegadon Mission Room and other places were more supernatural. I believe that very soon we shall witness the same in England.

Warmly welcomed by the pastor and his co-workers, I sat, of necessity, on the low, large platform, with its table and four forms. The room was an upper chamber, down a court out of a busy street.

It was very bare, with forms without any backs. But the enthusiastic congregation did not think of comfort.

Boys and girls around me, from seven to twelve years of age, were seeing visions and speaking in tongues—as well as older folk.

A bright-faced lad cried out with intense vehemence (eyes closed, right hand on heart, left hand stretched out)— "Oh...I see the house of Satan thrust down...and now the host are entering Heaven. Oh!...they are going to shut the door! and some will be too late. Oh! Jesus. Jesus." Then he commenced to shout in a rapid unknown tongue, and a few minutes later he was just a simple, lovable Norwegian boy again.

Then a university student (under the power of the Spirit) cries with great vehemence (to the "Djarvlen"), "Go...Will you go!...Will you go!" All this time perhaps a dozen are speaking or praying in Tongues, or prophesying, and prayer and praise "in the Spirit" is going on all over. Then suddenly a high-pitched musical voice is heard cutting into every-thing—prolonged, and then dying away. It is a woman prais-ing Christ in the Spirit.

A brother on my left breaks out into Tongues; three times in that meeting he did the same. First it seems to be in English, very rapidly spoken: "Come, come, come, come now to the Savior," etc. Then it seems to be like Chinese: "Chung, chew, chow," etc., Then he changes into a chat-tering sort of Tongue. I am assured that all there are Holy Ghost people. "The flesh may get in a little," says the good pastor, "but not much."

"TONGUES" AT KEWSICK
People of course, ridicule; but those meetings go on every day, and twice a day, and not in one place of meeting only nor in one single town. At Christiansand and Frederick-shaldt and many other places the same is going on, and it spreads quickly from each person who receives the Gift!

A Christian merchant in a high position in Denmark came with others to see and hear, and he told me that he was convinced it is of God. The working people chiefly fill the meetings, and the difficulty is to get them to leave when the time comes to close.

And, it must be added, practical results follow these strange meetings.

Pastor Barratt (of whom more below) said that till recently it was difficult to attract to religious meetings. A Salvation Army officer adver-tised that a man would rise from his coffin and preach the Gospel, but even this did not effectively draw. But now twice a day and every day and week after week these meetings are thronged by enthusiastic crowds, who go out to spread the strange flame, which they are convinced is Pentecostal and Heavenly and Scriptural.

The meetings are liable at any moment to be swept by a wave of spiritual power sweep-ing through all human arrange-ments. At times the noise is strangely awesome, almost appalling to an "outsider."

Some of us ask ourselves the question, how will this

affect the Keswick Convention meetings and other gatherings this year? Those who have "Tongues" will be present, and unable and unwilling to control them when moved by the Spirit.

The Rev. Thomas Ball Barratt, the leader of this movement, is almost a Norwegian. He was fours years old when his Cornish parents brought him to Hardanger. Eventually he became a missioner of the Methodist Episcopal Church, but he has practically detached himself from any church ties, and the work he feels is his parish.

He was in New York last autumn when influences from the Los Angeles movement began to reach him, and he received a mighty "Pentecost," he witnessed to by "Tongues." A letter he wrote home stirred up the spirit of expectancy, and on his arrival the work immediately began, and on New Year's Day in Norway the revival commenced, and has continued ever since, and is spreading all the time.

Of my own inner experiences whilst in these meetings I must refrain from writing at this point, but I reverently thank God for the privilege of being present.

"He will guide you into all truth." We ought to take the Holy Ghost before any other teacher. We should have no teacher between us and the Holy Ghost.

Please write very plainly in sending in your address for the paper. Some letters have to go into the waste basket, because the addresses are illegible or incomplete. If any fail to get the paper, please let us know.

We send out papers free, but freewill offerings have come in to enable us to publish and send to all that ask for them.

We have been publishing 30,000 papers at an issue, and of this number 40,000 are printed.

Anyone desiring to distribute papers, has only to drop us a

card saying how many you can use to advantage, giving your address very plainly, and we will send by return mail or as quickly as possible.

A convention of Prayer is to be held at Alliance, Ohio. The saints from Akron, Cleveland, Canton, and East Liverpool will meet there, and it will no doubt be a time of great power and blessing. The date is March 30th.

TWO PAPERS IN ONE

This number six of the "Apostolic Faith" has been enlarged. It is a double paper, the February-March number. We have no stated time of publication but expect to get it out every month, the Lord willing. This time it has been unavoidably delayed. Many have been looking forward to it and wondering why it did not come before. We praise God for the privilege of sending it out now to hungry souls, and pray God that it will be a double blessing.

The Lord has been greatly enlarging the work. Stacks of letters come in which we have not been able to answer, but may our correspondents take this prayer as an answer, as our hands are so full of the precious work. We have received many blessed reports and testimonies which it has been hard to condense into this paper. Many precious letters had to be left out for lack of space.

THE PURCHASE OF THE AZUSA MISSION

The lot and buildings at 312 Azusa Street have been purchased by the Apostolic Faith Mission. Twelve Holy Ghost men have been elected as trustees, who hold the property.

We believe the Lord chose this spot for His work, for He has wonderfully poured out His Spirit in the mission, which started about a year ago from cottage prayer meetings where the Pentecost first fell. Now, through Spirit baptized ones who have gone out, and through papers published here, there has been raised up a mighty host. Praise God!

The property was purchased for $15,000, and $4,000 has already been paid down on it.

Any friends wishing to have a share in buying this Mission for the Lord may send offerings to Bro. Reuben Clark, who is secretary of the Board of Trustees. Address 312 Azusa St., Los Angeles.

It was necessary to buy this mission as a headquarters for the work, in order to hold it, as it would soon have been sold for other purposes. The situation is favorable, being centrally located and in surroundings where no one will be disturbed by prayers or shouts going up sometimes all night. Praise God! The Mission building was formerly a place of worship where souls had been saved years ago, and the spot thus made sacred; and during the past year, hundreds have been saved, sanctified, healed, and baptized with the Holy Ghost.

Seven

MANY WITNESSES TO THE POWER OF THE BLOOD AND OF THE HOLY GHOST, APRIL 1907

THE APOSTOLIC FAITH

"Earnestly contend for the faith which was once delivered unto the saints."—Jude 3

Vol. 1, No. 7, Los Angeles, Cal., April, 1907, Subscription Free

IN AFRICA

Monrovia, Liberia, Mar. 26.— We opened a ten day's meeting in a school house, and on the tenth night, the Lord came in mighty power! Two were baptized with the Holy Ghost and spoke in tongues. Ten here have received sanctification, and five are filled with the Holy Ghost and speaking in tongues. A brother and his household have been baptized with the Holy Ghost. God has called him to the ministry and he will be baptized Sunday the 30th of March. Have been holding meetings going on three months. The Lord is sending a crowd of the African natives to the meeting and He is working wonderfully with them. The house is filled with the natives every service and they are being saved and sanctified and filled with the Holy Ghost and healed of all manner of diseases. The Lord surely is working with the native Africans of this land. All the saints send love.

IN LONDON

Allerman Road, Brixton, London, S.W., March 18.—Words fail to express our gratitude to God for pouring out so wonderfully His blessed Spirit. We can read nothing else now but our Bible and the accounts of His glorious doings in your midst and elsewhere. The reading of it has intensified the deep hunger of soul in the few waiting upon God and seeking our Personal Pentecost here. A dear sister here, a mother of three little ones yielded herself fully to God and sought the baptism with the Holy Ghost. One night she waited upon God and at midnight the Holy Ghost came down upon her and gave her the witness of tongues. The next day while at prayer, I being with her, she had a mighty anointing and has spoken in two or three tongues. This was on January 9. She could not give utterance to the raptures of her soul in praising the "Bleeding Lamb," and talked to God sometimes in a loud voice praising and adoring Him in a new tongue. Glory to His holy name.

—J. Hinmers

IN CALCUTTA, INDIA

55 Creek Row—God is spreading Pentecost here in Calcutta, and thirteen or fourteen missionaries and other workers have received it. The Spirit is giving the interpretation, song and writing in tongues, and other wonderful manifestations of His presence among us. O we do praise Him that the way ever opened for us to come to India. I cannot tell you how the Word is opening. Have never seen a meeting in my life where God has given more wonderful power on his blessed Word. We are among Bible teachers, and they have the Word so stored away; but now the Spirit is putting life and power into it; which is wonderful to behold. Praise our precious Christ.

God has put quite a burden on my heart for India's hungry souls. The Spirit has groaned through my soul for hungry ones until the pain was like travail. Oh how grateful we are for His working with us in this needy field.

We enjoy the paper very much, in fact, much of it is read in the meetings, and all rejoice. The little paper was a forerunner for us. We came to find that its contents had made God's children hungry for the light to come to India, and when we arrived we found some waiting for their Pentecost. We found India ripe for this light, in fact the revival had already broken out among the natives, and some were speaking in tongues.

Miss Easton, the head of the American Women's Board of Missions, the oldest women's missionary board in India, has been baptized and is a power for God.

We learn that the power has broken out in Russia, also in

London.—Sister A. G. Garr

IN SWEDEN

Viby, April 2.—Peace be unto you! Glory to God and praise His Holy name for evermore. Glory to God for victory through the Blood of Christ! I am happy in Jesus Christ and glad for what He has been doing in Sweden. The Lord has wonderfully kept me every day. Praise the Lord! Glory! There are not about twelve preachers who have received the Holy Ghost with signs following, and a few hundred have been saved, many getting a clean heart. Some have been healed, and many of God's children have received the Holy Ghost. I am called to many places and the cry for help comes from all over Sweden. I am very busy every day going from place to place. There is strong opposition and talking about me, and writing in the papers even. Glory to God, my King, for that. Glory! Glory!

Tell the saints to love one another and keep united in love, and under the Blood every day, and humble. I am with you every day in the Spirit and praying for you all. Glory to my King for victory! God's people are going to be one soon. Glory!

Apr. 15th 48 Skofde, Sweden.—The Lord Jesus Christ has done wonderful things in the last days, saving hundreds, sanctifying many, and hundreds have received their Pentecost with signs following. Praise the Lord. Many have been healed. Here is much to do every day. Many seekers after God. Over a hundred at the altar some meetings. A few interpret what they speak in tongues, and even myself. One day I interpreted these words, "Be ye separate from the world, that ye may be one," and "Abide in My love," and "For Thy greatness and might does the earth tremble," and Matt. 28: 19, 20. The Lord has supplied all my needs. Glory to God.

Many churches have been stirred up here. I expect greater things yet. A few who can read the paper are very glad to read it and are getting blest by it. My love to all the saints.
—Andrew G. Johnson

IN BELLE VERNON, PA.

April 19th.—The Lord is working here in Belle Vernon. People are being healed, devils are being cast out in Jesus' name. People are being baptized with the Holy Ghost and speaking with other tongues.—J. F. Mitchell

IN BELLINGHAM, WASHINGTON

In Bellingham, Wash, the Pentecost has fallen, quite a number have received the baptism and they have a mission of their own. Fourteen converts have been baptized in the bay.

IN MOBILE, ALA.

Davis and Anne Street, April 28.—The Lord has been working wonderfully here the past two weeks. Souls have been justified, sanctified, and are receiving the baptism with the Holy Ghost. One who was a sinner was healed in our meeting and the next night got saved. Her mother got healed and received the Holy Ghost all at the same time. Praise the Lord for victory. —F. W. Williams

IN SOUTH CAROLINA

Alvin, S. C., April 19.—My wife and I have been in a six wonderful meetings of late in which quite a number of saints have received the baptism with the Holy Ghost, and all spoke with other tongues. Backsliders are being reclaimed and some honest souls being converted, quite a lot of sick ones being healed, and also many demon possessed persons are being delivered in Jesus's name from the power of Satan. Glory to God!—F. M. Britton

IN LINCOLN, PA.

April 10.—God is having His way with many of His children in this part of the country. A great many, in the midst of much opposition, are being baptized with the Holy Spirit and speaking in tongues, among them a number of young people and children. The work is spreading in and about Pittsburgh and Allegheny, in Homestead, Braddock, McKeesport, and other places in this vicinity. —J. T. Boddy, pastor Pentecost church

IN SAN ANTONIO, TEX.

425 N. Pine Street, April 13.— We are in the midst of a glorious meeting in this city. Ten have received Pentecost with the Bible evidence of speaking in tongues, and a number have been saved and sanctified. God has enabled us to create a widespread interest throughout the city, and the opposition is forming in a very formidable way, we know that our God is able to deliver. We are going forward in simple faith in Him.—Daniel C. O. Opperman

IN ALLEGHENY, PA.

216 E. Stockton Ave., April 16.—Join with us in praising Him for the outpouring of God's Spirit in Pentecostal power in the district of Pittsburg, Pa. We had heard of God's outpouring all over the world, so we began to seek God's best for ourselves. I saw that power came only through heart purity, so I yielded myself up to God's searching power and got a glimpse of "Calvary;" and then, praise God, the power fell with the signs following. Pentecost first fell in the third week of January and is still going on. Hallelujah. Almost every meeting there are some prostrated under the power and coming through. Almost every one that speaks in tongues gets the message that Jesus, is coming soon. He is just the same yesterday, today and forever. —M. R. C.

IN HONOLULU, HAWAII

March 18.—We are just holding up Jesus before this people, and God is doing the rest. We had quite a scene at the altar last night, when a demon possessed man who was kneeling at the altar was picked up by demon power, thrown over the altar rail on his head, and when we commanded them to come out of him they barked at us and said that they would not come out of him, but they were cast out in the Name of Jesus and the man was set free. A Salvation Army captain has received his Pentecost. He is a noble young man, and desires to labor with the Apostolic Faith Movement. We are believing for a great work in the Islands. Jesus is coming very soon. Hallelujah! —H. M. and A. E. Turney

IN DURHAM, N. C.

March 28.—"Some of the Lord's people here have received their Pentecost and spoken in tongues. Glory! A red hot meeting is now going on. Bro. Fulford, who has the gift of tongues, is leading it under the direction of the Holy Ghost. The saints are being baptized with the Spirit. I too have received Him and have spoken in some kind of a language, I know not what. It is glory here now. What we are now praying for is to have the nine gifts of the Spirit here in full operation. This city has been mightily stirred on account of the tongues. Nearly the whole of North Carolina is being stirred among the Holiness people, white and colored.—W. L. Fisher, Box 208

IN SPRINGBORO, PA.

April 26.—God is meeting us here in some very marked ways. Many have gotten clear in their experience of sanctifi-cation, a backslider came back last evening, others are just on the eve of Pentecost, five have gotten through. The town is stirred. They say it is a work of the devil, and fight me, but, oh, what victory God gives in the midst. The preachers turn out well to these meetings. I don't know them until someone points them out to me afterward, so they get hit very often. The Free Methodist preacher confessed yesterday he was not sanctified. I think he will soon get somewhere. He said he was afraid to say anything about this movement. He knows God is in it.—Ivey Campbell

IN DAYTON, O.

April 6.—"Oh, I praise God for the gift of the Spirit. There were some seeking it on the west side here, and when it came, some of them refused it and said it was of the devil, but I was simple enough to take God at His Word, and two of us received our Pentecost. I received it February 22. Bless the dear Lord. There was a little preacher that went to Akron, O., and reached his Pentecost,

returning to Dayton. There are about 25 have received Pentecost through God using him. God picked him up a drunken gambler and saved and sanctified him, and sent him out to preach, and when he got his Pentecost most of the church people rejected him. We are going through hard persecution and we are having a time to get a place to worship; but we are holding on to God. We need your prayers, we are only babies, but our God is able and we are trusting Him."
—Delia Powell, 303 Spitler Ave.

IN SAN DIEGO, CAL.

Praise God! The fire still burns, sinners coming home to God, believers being sanctified and baptized with the Holy Ghost, speaking with other tongues as the Spirit gives them utterance. We joined with you all of like precious faith on April 9th, and commemorated the anniversary of the Pentecostal outpouring in California. We had a most blessed and glorious day. Hallelujah! The streams of living water and salvation flowed, and glorious deliverance came to some precious souls. The tide is rising higher and higher, the conviction going deeper and deeper, and the way growing brighter day by day. Oh, Glory! Hallelujah! This little army is marching on to sure and glorious victory through the precious blood of the Lamb.—F. E. Hill

736 145th Street, April 6.— The dear Lord is wonderfully blessing the work here in San Diego. Last night we had a powerful meeting; two were slain under the power of God, three received their Pentecost with the Bible evidence. Sinners were crying to God for mercy, and the saints were wonderfully blessed. —G. H. Reilly

IN HOMESTEAD, PA.

The Pentecost has fallen in Homestead, Pa. The meeting began in the Christian and Missionary Alliance Hall, Jan. 11. The power of the Holy Ghost was felt from the first service and a deep digging up begun among the people who were willing to go with God at any cost. Restitution, apologies and repentance was the business of the meeting for the first six days and nights. In fact the state to which some were led seemed perilous at times, but with confidence in the leading of God and with hearts desirous of going all the way, there was scarcely a halt, till everything in the past life had been fully reviewed from a Pentecostal standpoint, and every crooked or questionable act adjusted. On the seventh day the walls began to fall, and people fell under the power of God. The baptism was first received by Sister Robinson, who laid under the power for some time, then came through speaking in tongues. The next night the husband received his Pentecost at his home, and spoke and sang in new tongues. From this on the work has been going forward with uninterrupted sway.

The hall soon became too small when we were compelled to secure a larger one in order to accommodate the increasing crowds.

Many have received their personal Pentecost and speak and sing in new tongues, and have power over demons to cast them out and to pray the prayer of faith for the healing of the sick.

For miles around people are coming in to investigate this work and to receive their Pentecost.—"The Latter Rain"

IN FORT WORTH, TEX. 1,005 Edward St., April 22. We have a small band here. Have been meeting in private houses asking the Lord to open a door for us that no man could shut. We are praising the Lord this morning that we have a tent paid for and lights and seats secured. O, how happy I am at the prospect. Just as soon as the weather clears away, we want to begin meetings. We are expecting our God to do great things, for when I read of the wonderful work at Azusa, my heart rejoices so that I fall to my knees to thank God. We want the heavenly showers to fall on us too. We have four now waiting for the promise of the Father. A young man, a preacher, came to see me last Tuesday. He said that a little more than four months ago he was down waiting on God for an infilling of the Holy Spirit, when after waiting on God he began to pray in language unknown to him. This came on him in a few days. He told his presiding elder, who said that was foolishness. He said that once after that he felt like letting the Lord have His way with him, but on account of discouragements he did not do so. When he came here he hunted us up, and the power all came back to him. He never had anyone to help or tell him about this great movement. —Mrs. C. A. Roll

IN TORONTO, CANADA

The Lord is wonderfully blessing the work in 651 Queens Street, E. Toronto. For five months it has gone on without a break. Nearly 80 have received the Baptism with the Holy Ghost, speaking in tongues. Four workers have gone out from here to preach the full Gospel. Many are being healed. Last Sunday we had a glorious time all day, especially in the afternoon service, when the power of God prostrated two brothers and came upon many at the altar. The whole meeting place was used as an altar, everyone turning their seats and getting down before the Lord. One brother who began speaking in tongues staggered to his feet exclaiming: "This is glory, glory, glory!" and before he had gone through a sister rose under the power of God and commenced saying: "This is glory, glory." A spirit of great rejoicing seized everyone. It was a time of magnifying God. Truly He has done great things. A band of workers from this mission went to a place just outside the city limits and held services, and the power of God came down upon the people. We are believing for a mighty outpouring upon the people in that district. —Sister Hebden

IN INDIANAPOLIS, IND.

2341 Fletcher Ave., April 20.—Praise God for ever and ever. It is wonderful how God is manifesting His power here in bringing dear souls through and healing the sick. This is stirring up the ministers and people, and the newspapers are lying and trying to put the people against us, but God is overruling and people who never dreamt of coming under the influence of God's power have been stricken down and are getting salvation, their baptism and speaking in tongues.

Yesterday afternoon God took a young colored brother and a young sister, and in a most marvelous manner the Holy Spirit spoke through them in tongues, giving the interpretation, and with such power and force that the whole audience was stricken with awe. Weeping was seen all over the place, and they acknowledge it was God and the power of the Holy Ghost. There must have been a dozen ministers or more present, and one of them the leading ministers of this city. He was advertised to preach against us next Sunday, April 21; but, thank God, he and his wife wept with the rest. When I asked: Is there a man or woman who dare stand up and say these children were hypocrites? this same minister said: "No, it is God."

One man who did not know anything about the meetings, but saw the sign as he was passing, came in out of curiosity. He is a doctor and medical nurse, has spent some time in India, and can talk in many of the Indian languages. He said he was surprised soon after he had taken his seat, then God struck him and he was brought under deep conviction. It kept increasing. He got desperate. God kept telling him to go to the penitent form. He did not want to for fear he would be laid out upon the floor. He got more desperate, until he bought some poison, and if he did not get through last Thursday afternoon he intended taking the poison. He had not slept any since last Sunday night. Praise God, he came and went through and got the whole thing. When he received his baptism he threw up his hands, gave a shout of Glory, and over he went backwards upon the floor. While there, Jesus came to him and told him He wanted him to return to India and preach the Gospel. He promised he would

and take others with him, if it is His will. Glory to our Christ for ever and ever. He identified one of the tongues spoken by a young sister and told us it was the Marathi language. He also identified other languages in others. He had to give up all his business before God would receive him, and go to the medical staff and tell them what for. Our only desire and heart's cry is: Precious souls for Jesus and heaven.
—T. Hezmalhalch

Eight

Los Angeles Campmeeting of the Apostolic Faith Missions, May 1907

The Apostolic Faith

"Earnestly contend for the faith which was once delivered unto the saints."—Jude 3

Vol. 1, No. 8, Los Angeles, Cal., May, 1907, Subscription Free

We expect to have a grand campmeeting in Los Angeles, beginning June 1, and continuing about four months.

The spot selected for it is adjoining the city limits, several miles from the center of town in a grove of sycamore and live oak trees near Hermon. The fare is only five cents on the electric cars which run every seven minutes. It is only three blocks from where the cars stop to the campmeeting.

We expect to have a tabernacle with seating capacity of about 1,000 people. There will be room in the grove for many tents. Free camping grounds. The air is fresh with the sea breeze which comes in from the distant ocean, and there is plenty of good water. You can pray there as loud as you like. There are wooded hills all about which we expect will ring with the songs and prayers of the saints and shouts of newborn souls.

There will be a separate tabernacle for meetings for the children with services daily, so it will be a children's campmeeting as well as a grown-up people's meeting. There will be competent workers to teach and help them spiritually. We expect it to be a time of salvation among the children. Mother's meetings are also planned for.

Workers from all missions in and about Los Angeles who are one with us, by virtue of having been baptized by one Spirit into one body, are uniting in this campmeeting. Services will be continued in Azusa Mission every night just the same as ever, a band going from the camp-meeting to carry on the work. Other missions will also carry on their work.

A large band of Holy Ghost workers, men and women whom God has equipped for His service will be present to carry on the meeting, under the guidance of our blessed Redeemer whom we honor as the great Leader and Manager. Much prayer is going up to God that He will make this a time of visiting His people with salvation and an outpouring of Pentecost such as we have never witnessed before. The business part of the work is being arranged in orderly and systematic shape. Proper officers will have charge of the grounds, putting up tents, etc.

The workers from the different missions first met to counsel together about the campmeeting. We got down to ask the Lord for the money, and the witness came that prayer was heard; the Spirit was poured out upon us. We arose and decided to lease the ground for four months. Before the meeting was over, the power of God so filled the room that one fell under the power and the meeting turned into a Pentecostal service.

A number are willing giving their services in clearing and preparing the grounds. No collections have been taken, but several hundred dollars have already been offered for the campmeeting. God hears prayer and is putting His seal on it.

VIEWING THE CAMPGROUND

Last summer during the hot days when the crowds would fill the Azusa Mission all day, people would often get up and say they praised God for what He was doing for them "this morning;" not realizing that the sun was going down in the evening. They had not eaten all day and yet they were so taken up with sitting at the feet of Jesus that they lost track of the time and would sit there in the heat, wiping the perspiration from their faces. I thought how God was pleased with it, and how He would be pleased to give them a nice shady place in which to worship.

A few weeks later, as our sister was reading the letters on Sunday morning in Azusa Mission from the foreign lands and the homeland, as she was reading about a campmeeting in the east, she said she believed the Lord would give us a campmeeting here. The Lord began to talk to me about the campmeeting. He talked to me during the night and the next morning the burden of the campmeeting was so on my heart, that I laid aside my work and went over to the Mission and asked our sister if the Lord had laid it on her heart where He was going to have the campmeeting. It seemed to me that morning I could see in a vision the grove and the little white tents all through it. And God was showing us both the same spot. While we were talking, a brother came in with the burden of the campmeeting on his heart. He had not been able to sleep for thinking of it and where to have it. We said we would all go and view the grounds, so a company of us started.

As we landed there, every step we took seemed to praise God. The very trees seemed to clap their hands and say "Praise God." As we walked down the Arroyo, heaven came down our souls to greet, and we said, "Surely God is in it." We began to get thirsty and went to a sister's house to get a drink from the well in her yard. She came out rejoicing, seeking her Pentecost. As we began to drink we thought of how God will water thirsty souls there, and we sang, "By Samaria's wayside well, once a blessed message fell, On a woman's thirsty soul long ago." And the power of God came upon us all. We went back and viewed the ground again. Surely it looks like the hand of Beulah around there. We went on and visited a dear old brother in Hermon and he rejoiced at the prospect of the campmeeting. All welcomed us and praised God. —One of the Committee.

Arrangements are being made for reduced rates on all lines of railroad for those coming to the campmeeting.

On arriving in Los Angeles, take the South Pasadena or Church of Angels car, and get off at Sixtieth Ave.

Tents can be purchased or rented at reasonable prices on the camp ground. Bring with you necessary provision for living in tents.

For full information in regard to the campmeeting, address Apostolic Faith Campmeeting, 312 Azusa St., Los Angeles, Cal.

PENTECOSTAL MEETINGS
IN LITTLE ROCK, ARK.

May 7.—I thank God that I am able to report victory through Jesus Christ our Lord. We are now in the midst of a great meeting. The fire is fall-ing and the people are getting the baptism right along. The Holy Ghost is working in our midst as never before. The Lord has made known to us that the speaking in tongues is the Bible evidence of the baptism with the Holy Ghost. Bro. Jeter and I are holding the meeting here with some others of the brethren. Pray much that we may get out of the way of the Holy Ghost, so that He can run things to suit Himself. —D. J. Young, 212 N. Hickory St., Pine Bluff, Ark.

IN TOPEKA, KANSAS

Mission, 926 N. Kans. Ave., May 9.—It is surely wonderful how the Lord is working all over the world, and I am glad I have a part in this great work. Praise His name. The work here is moving ahead and several are tarrying and seeking Pentecost. A half dozen or more have received the baptism and have spoken in tongues. Sister Culp has returned to us from Los Angeles, where she received her Pentecost. God is using her here to His glory in speaking in tongues and telling of His wonderful works. We had a blessed day Sunday. The afternoon service ran on into the night. The power of God came on one sister. She got up from the altar and shouted all over the house and praised God. Her husband went down on his back under the power. He said he was nearer the Lord than he had ever been. Others are earnestly seeking. The devil is fighting hard, but we are determined to stay on the field and let God have His way with us.—C. E. Foster

IN CHICAGO, ILL.

943 W. North Ave., April 11.—Our meetings are wonderful, indeed, since I received my Pentecost. From the first day I arrived home, the mission will not hold the people, and I have moved out of the rooms in the rear of the Mission and we use them for overflow and prayer rooms, and still we cannot accommodate the crowds on Sunday. Best of all, the Spirit works in mighty power, and people fall under it, and many have come through and spoken in tongues. My dear wife received her Pentecost soon after I reached home, and

yesterday one of our elders, who had been seeking for months, came through. Hallelujah! People are coming from all directions, and the interest and power is increasing daily, until I never saw more of the power of God anywhere than we see here from time to time. Best of all it is all of God— no one can claim any credit— God just comes with power and takes possession.

We never forget to pray for Azusa St. Mission, and hope you remember us. Beloved, let us walk in meekness before the Lord, and give Him the glory for what He is doing, and He will be with us. I feel like staying at His feet all the time.

April 13.—It is wonderful how He is working in our midst. One after another are coming through and speaking in tongues. Last night the meeting lasted all night.

IN MEMPHIS, TENN.

May 2.—The Lord our God is with us at this place, and the saints are receiving their Pentecost. I have never met with such power of the devil as here. One man came to the service and dragged his wife from the altar by force and threatened to kill me and others. But, glory to God, he was overpowered by our God. His wife got the baptism and spoke in tongues, and last night he was back to the service and says he must have his Pentecost. Praise God. I heard from Bro. Mason's church. The power is falling and many souls being filled and speaking in tongues. I met Bro. Mason last week and found him willed with the blessed Holy Ghost. He is a precious brother. Here is a battle but our God is fighting it for us. We are only here to stand still and see the salvation of the Lord. The saints are gathering here from Mississippi, Missouri and points in Tennessee. This work at Memphis is now on footing to continue all summer. I long to see you all in life, but if not I will meet you at the marriage supper of the Lamb. —G. B. Cashwell

In Alliance, O.

We are in the midst of a gracious outpouring of God's Spirit in our ten days consecration: people are coming up as they did to Jerusalem, anxious to know the way of God more perfectly. Thirteen were laid out under the power at once, some who had had their Pentecost receiving prophecy, many sweet heavenly messages. A young Irish boy, 20 years an orphan, was saved on the vessel two years ago as Rev. Lupton was on his way to Africa. He came to the Home here two weeks ago and received Pentecost in a few days. God has been so marvelously using him and making him such a blessing to all. He prophesied under the power more than six hours. He was telling of the countries of Africa, and spoke of many of the places Rev. Lupton has visited. The boy himself was never in Africa, but was on his way to England when converted.

A doctor from Oberlin College arose in the meeting while Rev. McKenney was giving the message and said: "I believe it, I have been skeptical, but I do know it is true." The altar filled at once with men. Some women knelt at the front seats. Oh, how we love to honor the precious Blood. It is so blessed to stand and see the salvation of God. We count the Holy Ghost faithful.

A very large company of us are enjoying Pentecost now in Ohio. It is spreading rapidly. We are getting many urgent calls. Pray much for the laborers. The devil is hard after us.—I. C.

IN MINNEAPOLIS

320 S. Cedar St., April 15.— Yesterday, our first Sunday, was a day of great victory for the Lord. At the afternoon and evening services, the altar was crowded with earnest, anxious seekers—between fifty and sixty last night. I feel that God is going to sweep Minneapolis as she was never swept before. Glory! We are giving the strong meat of the Word, preaching repentance and restitution as the only foundation upon which the Holy Ghost will build; and it is taking. The Dowieites are closing up their missions and coming with us. We have a large hall, and it was filled all

day yesterday. Hallelujah.

May 3. This is a blessed day after our great victory of last night. One sister received her Pentecost and talked for some time in tongues. Some understood her when she spoke in Polish and others recognized several sentences spoken in Bohemian. I recognized the Chinese when she spoke that and another recognized the Italian. She sang beautifully in the Norwegian tongue. Of course the devil was stirred and there were threats of throwing me in jail because someone suggested hypnotism. We are having wonderful meetings. Bro. Pendleton felt the presence of the Holy Ghost fire as I did at the beginning of the meeting last night. He had no sermon. We went to the altar after singing a couple of songs. The Swedish sisters are with us. Their ship sails May 17. They are blessed women of God. —J. R. Conlee

IN DENVER, COLO.

1312 Wellton St., March 18.—Sinners are being saved, believers are being sanctified and baptized with the Holy

Ghost and fire and speaking in tongues. The altar is full of seekers every afternoon and evening, and people are being healed of scrofula, salt rheum, curvature of the spine, locomotive ataxia, diseases of the eyes, ears, etc.

One lady had a legion of demons cast out of her, was saved, sanctified and baptized with the Holy Ghost inside an hour, and spoke in tongues at the night meeting. One Swedish young man here had a demon cast out and received the baptism with the Holy Ghost, speaking in tongues, inside of two and a half hours.

People of all ages with all manner of diseases are coming for healing, and the deaf, lame and blind. The Acts of the Apostles are being repeated here now. Handkerchiefs are being blessed and sent to sick people in other places, and children of God are getting handkerchiefs blessed for unbelieving husbands and children and for sick folks here in and around Denver. This gives an outline of the work going on here the past two or three weeks. I want to tell you also that God sends in an interpreter from time to time. One night here a young cowboy from the Creek Indians dropped in and heard one of the sisters speaking the Creek Indian language, and another night a doctor dropped in who understood three languages she spoke.— Mrs. Nora Wilcox

PENTECOST IN ENGLAND
The brother who went from England to investigate the work in Norway, Bro. A. A. Boddy, All Saints' Vicarage, Monkwearmouth, Sunderland, England, sent out the following in tract form:

SPEAKING IN TONGUES.
IS THIS OF GOD?
In the spring and summer of 1906, God began to answer the very prolonged cry of some of His hungry children, a cry for a Pentecost with scripture evidences.

One after another became at last conscious, as the mighty power of God came upon them, that they were speaking in divine ecstacy with a voice that was not their own, and in a language whether of men and angels they knew not, for until some received the gift of interpretation it was not known what they said. They were speaking mysteries to God for their own strengthening. (1 Cor., xiv., 2–4.)

The work which the writer believes was of God then came nearer to us. He, himself, has heard (this year, 1907) numbers of Spirit-filled men and women and even children magnifying God in tongues. They were all trusting in the Work of the Cross, adoring the Crucified; and sinners were being converted. He was in eight meetings, and he praises God with full heart for that fellowship. He can witness that all are strengthened by the knowledge that the Holy Ghost has come into fuller possession, they are filled with joy unspeakable and full of glory. But God is now graciously working in our midst with the signs and gifts.

The writer can testify as a rejoicing witness. He could write of very strange things. Earnest prayer which has ascended for months has been gloriously answered and greater things are yet to happen. Glory to the Lamb with Seven Horns and Seven Eyes! May we ever keep true to Him and hidden in Him (Rev. v. 6; Col. iii. 3).

GOD IS GIRDING THE WHOLE WORLD WITH THIS SIGN OF HIS OUT-POURING OF THE SPIRIT

A letter from another part of our own band says:

"Our sister and two or three others have been seeking for months. She got so hungry that it came to a point of real travail of soul, after which came a rest of faith, joy and peace. Not long after this (about three weeks) while about her domestic work, the Holy Ghost came upon her, and she spoke a few utterances in tongues, and as time went on it became more fluent. Our brother who has recently received was praising the Lamb of God (under the power of the Spirit) when he began a song without words for a time (worshipping in the Spirit) then a few utterances in tongues, and so on till he spoke most fluently. I can say from experience that we have a terrible battle with the powers of Hell, but we are learning to claim the victory through the Blood, and the Lord is teaching us to let all go into His Hands."

The wonderful sign in 1906 is the restoration of tongues, which foretells the preaching of the pure gospel to all nations, which must be done before the Gentile Times end. (Matt. 24:14.)—The Prophetic Age

-----

You do not have to strain your mind in order to receive the Holy Ghost, but just believe the Word of Jesus and the Lord pours the Holy Ghost into your heart just as freely as the air you breathe.

What the people need today is an experimental salvation wrought out in their hearts, we have something that will stand against all the forces and powers of hell. God is our life. He is our all in all, it is Christ the Son of the living God.

The "Vanguard" people in St. Louis are waiting on God for the outpouring of the Spirit, and one brother has received the baptism of the Holy Ghost and is speaking in tongues. Their paper is now called "The Banner of Truth."

A Norwegian brother in Brooklyn, New York, was reading about the Pentecost in Christiana when he was baptized with the Holy Ghost and began to speak in different languages. It was about midnight on January 26. His name is Oscar Halvorsen of 293 13th Street. Three others in Brooklyn are speaking in tongues.

MUSIC FROM HEAVEN

It has been often related how the Pentecost fell in Los Angeles over a year ago in a cottage prayer meeting. Sister Jennie Moore who was in that meeting and received her Pentecost gives her testimony as follows:

"For years before this wonderful experience came to us, we as a family, were seeking to know the fulness of God, and He was filling us with His presence until we could hardly contain the power. I had never seen a vision in my life, but one day as we prayed there passed before me three white cards, each with two names thereon, and but for fear I could have given them, as I saw every letter distinctly. On April 9, 1906, I was praising the Lord from the depths of my heart at home, and when the evening came and we attended the meeting the power of God fell and I was baptized in the Holy Ghost and fire, with the evidence of speaking in tongues. During the day I had told the Father that although I wanted to sing under the power I was willing to do whatever He willed, and at the meeting when the power came on me I was reminded of the three cards which had passed me in the vision months ago. As I thought thereon and looked to God, it seemed as if a vessel broke within me and water surged up through my being, which when it reached my mouth came out in a torrent of speech in the languages which

God had given me. I remembered the names on the cards: French, Spanish, Latin, Greek, Hebrew, Hindustani, and as the message came with power, so quick that but few words would have been recognized, interpretation of each message followed in English, the name of the language would come to me. I sang under the power of the Spirit in many languages, the interpretation both words and music which I had never before heard, and in the home where the meeting was being held, the Spirit led me to the piano, where I played and sang under inspiration, although I had not learned to play. In these ways God is continuing to use me to His glory ever since that wonderful day, and I praise Him for the privilege of being a witness for Him under the Holy Ghost's power." —J. M., 312 Azusa St., Los Angeles.

The interpretation of many of the messages in nearly every language spoken by the Holy Ghost in unknown tongues is that Jesus is coming.

Nine

In the Last Days,
June–September 1907

The Apostolic Faith

"Earnestly contend for the faith which was once delivered unto
the saints."—Jude 3

Vol. 1, No. 9, Los Angeles, Cal., June to September, 1907, Subscription Free

"AND IT SHALL COME TO PASS IN THE LAST DAYS, SAITH THE LORD, I WILL POUR OUT OF MY SPIRIT UPON ALL FLESH."—ACTS 2:17

THE REVIVAL IN PORTLAND

One of the mightiest revivals that Portland ever knew has taken place in that city. The devil raged, shots were fired, some were arrested and brought up before the judges, but the Lord worked on and healed all manner of diseases that were brought, baptized and saved many precious souls.

One poor soul that had spent five years strapped to her bed in an insane asylum was healed. Her brother hearing of the wonderful work wrought through this people went and got her and brought her to the Mission, and God wonderfully healed and saved and sanctified her. Her brother testified that he did not believe in God and was an infidel. Now he is saved and has gone back to live with his wife he had left. This Gospel surely is building homes.

A lady was instantly healed of lesion of the muscles which the doctors have been working on for eleven years. The saints are leaving off their glasses and their eyes are being instantly healed. An old lady well on to seventy years old had her eyes completely restored while listening to a brother preaching.

When the plague in Portland was taking the children off at a fearful rate, the Lord healed all the Pentecostal flock as soon as it put in its appearance. Not one of them lost one of their family. The people were told to read the 91st Psalm, stand on the Word, and fear nothing.

The Portland campmeeting

opened at Twelfth and Division Streets with 1,000 people in attendance, sometimes hundreds could not get in. They had all things common at the camp, and such love and unity exists. The poor saint could have a tent as well as the rich one and all were free to eat at the tables. No collections were taken, and yet the needs were abundantly supplied.

The work is spreading. Some came from Dallas and received their baptism and went back and set that town on fire and started a campmeeting there.

Sixty-seven were baptized in water one day. People brought their dear ones from the asylum and God healed them. Three from the asylum testified daily of the healing power of God.

A sanctified Nazarene preacher came to the meeting and got her baptism. Three preachers got through one day. The altars are packed.

A sister writing from there said, "O I wish you could hear these Holy Ghost people testify. No straps on anyone. The Holy Ghost works here. Saints filled so they can hardly talk jump up quickly, say a few words and sit down. Such a humble people, such love and unity I never saw.—Pentecostal Meeting, Twelfth and Division Streets, Portland, Ore.

THE "LATTER RAIN" IN ZION CITY, ILL.

God is doing a mighty work in Zion City among those heartbroken and crushed people. First they started meetings in the Edina Hospice, now a faith home called "The Haven," then they had the large auditorium in the college and now have the large tabernacle.

One morning in the upper room of "The Haven" the Holy Ghost fell, as they were praying for Him to come and manifest Himself. First one began to drop and then another until the floor was covered. The first to speak in unknown tongues was a young men who spoke in Chinese, Italian, and Zulu, which were identified. Then it was not long till the flood of joy began and all over the room they were praising and glorifying God in different tongues. Some were justified and sanctified. About twenty came through speaking in tongues.

God is using the children, young men and young women, in a marvelous manner. It is the most wonderful demonstration of the power of God upon human hearts. Denounce it as they will, when they see these little children under the power of the Holy Spirit, preaching, singing and speaking in different languages (which are many times identified by foreigners) they will in our meetings confess that their fighting has come to an end, and say that they have never seen anything after this manner.

Brother Seymour when he was in Zion City wrote, "People here receive the baptism in their pews while the service is going on and sometimes scores of them receive it. It is the sweetest thing you want to see. It reminds me of old Azusa ten months ago. The people that receive the baptism seem so happy, they remind of our people at home. There are little children from six years and on up who have the baptism with the Holy Ghost, just as we have it in Los Angeles. Praise our God. This is another Azusa. It would do you good to hear these people speak under the power of the Holy Ghost. Some of them converse in tongues. Brother Tom has never lost the spirit of Azusa. He is still fired up the same as ever. Everywhere I have traveled among our baptized souls they seem to have such joy and freedom in the Holy Ghost."— "The Haven," Zion City, Ill.

IN MINNEAPOLIS, MINN. One Sunday the power of God came upon us in the morning meeting and in the evening the Pentecost began to fall, and by 11:30 the next morning six had received Pentecost. "For they heard them speak with tongues and magnify God." It was like some scenes in Azusa, all around lay the slain, Methodists, Baptists, and Lutherans. Young people arose with shining faces speaking in the power of the Holy Ghost in unknown tongues. Two elderly sisters also spoke in tongues, magnifying God. We have the happiest band of baptized people you ever saw. Young ladies that were so timid, now clap their hands and shout Glory, all the time.

Another night, when the meeting lasted till five o'clock in the morning, one young man, a Methodist, came through about one a. m. and spoke in tongues for two hours, giving some of the most blessed messages and interpreting: the burden was, "Jesus is coming soon, get ready to meet Him."

One little girl received her baptism and spoke beautifully in tongues, and had then spoke to some unconverted young men in tongues and interpreted, which was a plea for them to give their hearts to Jesus now as He was soon coming and they would be lost. The men were visably affected by the message.

Three baptismal services were held (up to June 19th) at a suburban lake, and 24 were buried in the likeness of His death.

Most of those who received the baptism of the Spirit are prostrated on the floor. Some received it while sitting in a chair or standing on their feet. Some have received it at home.

Those who are prostrated, many of them tell of having a vision of heaven or of Jesus the Lord or otherwise of having come into a full and far deeper sense of God than ever thought or before. A brother coming out from under the power where he had received revelations said, "The hand of God is certainly on this work, and those who scoff and oppose it are likely to have the Lord's hand put on them in a terrible way."

The papers published many false reports, and they were threatened with arrest and to have the meetings stopped on the charge of disturbing the peace; but Bro. Pendleton announced that the meetings would continue for they must obey God. If they went to jail, they would have meetings there.

Some get to God in every meeting. They obtained a large hall that will set four or five hundred, where a permanent mission will be established.

PENTECOST IN WINNIPEG, MANITOBA

For more than a year here some of the saints tarried before God for an outpouring of His Spirit upon all flesh, and especially for a revival of the Bible standard in Winnipeg. God has heard prayers and is repeating Pentecost. Praise His name.

The Holy Ghost first fell in a cottage meeting and three received their Pentecost with Bible evidence. An aged saint came in from Poplar Point, a small town about 40 miles distant, and the second afternoon he got his Pentecost and says he feels a lot younger. He and others went back and had tarrying meetings, and since then about twenty have received Pentecost at that place.

At the Pentecost Mission, while a brother was speaking from Acts 10:40–46, "While Peter yet spake these words, the Holy Ghost fell on all them which heard the Word," as he was speaking, the Holy Ghost fell on two sisters. One started speaking right off in tongues, and another who had come about 100 miles to attend the meeting, fell under the power for a time and began to sing in tongues. It was heavenly. Souls are being saved, believers sanctified and baptized with the Holy Ghost while sitting in their seats.

Baptismal services took place on the banks of the River Assimboine. At this place 23 persons received baptism by immersion. It was a sacred occasion. The Holy Ghost witnessed through the speaking in tongues of those who were baptized.

Some wonderful cases of healing have occurred the past few weeks. A lady of some 60 years of age who had been a cripple from inflammatory rheumatism for ten years or more, was brought in an invalid chair accompanied by her two daughters. She was prayed for, and during the service was noticed to stretch forth her ailing limbs, which up to this time had been of little use to her. She then rose from her chair under the power of the Holy Ghost. O that men would praise the Lord for His goodness and His wonderful works to the children of men.— Home & Foreign Mission, 159 Alexander St., Winnipeg, Man., Can.

FROM DISTANT LANDS

How wonderful it is that today in different parts of India, Russia, Norway, Sweden, England, Canada, Africa and America, God's saints are enjoying the latter rain and are being satisfied. Persecution is arising everywhere, but this is only a mark of the Lord's work, and makes us more sure we shall reign with Him whose sufferings we are privileged to share. Bless His name! The Lord is coming—our precious King is coming soon. "Even so come Lord Jesus." Hallelujah.

SALVATION IN SWEDEN

In Stockholm, Sweden, many souls are filled with the Holy Ghost and have the Bible evidence. The tidal wave is sweeping on, on to victory. Hundreds of souls are at the feet of Jesus.

"The work of the Lord is spreading. In Gottenberg, the second city of Sweden, the Lord has set many of His people free, filling them with the Spirit of Christ. Some are speaking with new tongues. I have Bro. Eric Hollingsworth and his wife here with me now in this city, and hope we shall have a house like Azusa Mission.

"The church in Skofde is growing. I think there are about 40 now who are baptized with the Holy Ghost and speaking and singing in new tongues there. Hallelujah! In a meeting at Skofde there were seven young folks who were singing in tongues together. It was a heavenly song, as Bro. Eric told me.

"In many other cities and towns God is working mightily. One place is on an island between Sweden and Russia, and God is pouring out His Spirit. To God be all the praise."—Andrew G. Johnson, Bramaregarden, Hisingstad, Gottenberg, Sweden

[Since the last report, two Spirit-filled sisters, Sister Anderson and Sister Jacobson, have gone to help in the work in Sweden.]

REPORTS FROM ENGLAND

"Three have received the baptism with Bible evidence here. When we hear the Holy Ghost speaking and singing through these dear ones, it is

so solemn and yet so heavenly and deepens one's hunger."
—J. H. 14 Akerman Road, Brixton, London, S. W.

From another part of London where there has been a tarrying meeting, word comes that two have received the Pentecost, and other hungry souls are seeking.

A sister in England who has received the Holy Ghost testifies:

"When all had retired that night, past twelve o'clock, and I was left alone, praise and adoration filled my soul (for the words kept ringing in my ear that had been spoken from, 'Faithful is He that calleth you, who also will do it.') The joy was flowing—after months of inexpressible yearnings and waiting upon God. That night I seemed to lie down in His almighty arms like a weary, little child. The last cord that bound me to earth was broken and that was a little anxiety concerning my home and dear ones. I gave them up to Him, and just rested absolutely in Him.

"While praising Him I had a vision of Jesus upon the cross. It was dark. He extended His arms to me and said, 'Come to Me.' Oh! The unutterable love and compassion in His voice. I obeyed, and groaned in the spirit, seeming to suffer with Him. Then the darkness fled, and I was raised with Him in glory. I involuntarily threw up my arms to praise Him and suddenly they seemed to be charged with electricity, and a power came upon me and I praised Him in another tongue. He immediately gave the interpretation which was 'Glory to Jesus—the bleeding Lamb.' The next morning the Holy Ghost came in mighty power, causing me to laugh as I had never done in my life (being very matter of fact and unemotional), and speaking in four or five languages sometimes giving the interpretation. For one and a half hours this continued. I was quite powerless. The glory of God filled my soul, and sometimes the deepest anguish of heart at the cross. What I felt and realized of the sorrow and love of Jesus was beyond all expression, finding vent only in another 'tongue.' Glory to His Name!

"The same evening I went to another meeting in connection with the foregoing special services, and the Spirit came upon me again causing me to speak in three or four languages with the interpretation."

—Bro. A. A. Body, All Saints' Vicarage, Monkwearmouth, Sunderland, England

THE WORK IN INDIA

There are at least five or six hundred witnesses in India today, "earnestly contending for the faith once delivered unto the saints."

Some of the choicest spirits of India have been baptized with the Holy Ghost. It is wonderful to hear one of these tell how for nine years she had hunted meetings where she could receive the Holy Ghost, and how she has found Him whom her soul so long has craved. She and her friend are missionaries from Colombo, Ceylon. One of them has been clearly healed of a disease of several years standing.

Four witnesses have gone to Darjeeling, India.

A prominent missionary who has been baptized with the Holy Ghost and has received wonderful power has thrown open the doors of her beautiful mission home and today is preaching the word with power.

The missionaries are searching the Word. They find this movement is prophesied as the forerunner of Jesus, and the precious souls are so glad to receive the power; but in India Bible teachers who know the Word are not jumping at every new doctrine but are weighing everything by the Word and are being convinced of the truth.

The Lord gave one missionary a vision of the Holy Ghost as a chest of jewels, and she saw the Savior open the chest, and with a look of great love and satisfaction, unroll gift after gift from the chest. It has not occurred to many the joy that must fill the heart of the dear Lord, when He sees that His gifts are being appreciated.

The Lord also gave Sister Garr a vision of Himself one night, while in Calcutta and

His hands were filled with golden crowns ready to place on heads. And the same evening, He gave her the message "Let no man take thy crown." A missionary arose and said that on that day God had spoken those words to her, and she did not know what it meant.

Reaching the missionaries is laying the axe at the root of the tree, for they know all the customs of India and also the languages. The only way the nations can be reached is by getting the missionaries baptized with the Holy Ghost. Missionaries are receiving and praising God for letting them hear this Gospel and receive this great outpouring of the Spirit.

In a school of 1,500 native girls and 200 boys, besides European and native teachers, the head of the school has been tarrying and the Comforter has come to her and also to her daughter, a number of her teachers, and 300 native girls. Hallelujah! At Dhond, a school of boys, numbers have been saved, some are speaking in tongues.

In Calcutta, one Missionary who was baptized in the meeting went back to her high school and in a short time forty-five precious native girls were baptized in the Spirit. Then the matron of a Rescue Home received her Pentecost and shortly the dear girls who had been redeemed from such lives of sin, were learning how to glory Jesus and the Holy Ghost was given. Missionaries who have gone down to their stations, write of the abiding Comforter and rivers of living water are flowing.

False reports have been circulated of the work in India. Do not believe them. —Bro. and Sister A. G. Garr, Bethany, Slave Island, Colombo, Ceylon, India

-----

When Jesus comes, he is going to reveal to us, all the hidden love that He had for us all through the ages.

If your testimony is backed up by the Blood of Christ in your heart, there is power in it.

God stands today to save every sinner, to sanctify every believer, and to baptize every sanctified believer with the Holy Ghost.

We are measuring everything by the Word, every experience must measure up with the Bible. Some say that is going too far, but if we have lived too close to the Word, we will settle with the Lord when we meet Him in the air.

When we preach a sinless life, some people say we are too strict. They say we will not get many to heaven that way. But beloved, God cannot save contrary to His Word. All salvation contrary to the Word is not saving salvation.

The baptism with the Holy Ghost is the seal of the living God in your forehead. God wants you to wear this seal, and not the badges of men and devils. He does not want you to be unequally yoked together with unbelievers, but come out from among the creeds and doctrines of men and devils. Our ignorance in the past God winked at, but that time is past. He is seeking for a clean people, a people that have not defiled their garments. The priests that bore the holy vessels had to be clean, so now those that bear the messages of the Lord must be clean and holy.

John the Baptist lost his head because he preached against divorces. There are a few people today that are willing to lose their heads for preaching against divorces. This Apostolic Faith stands for one wife and one husband. Our God is going to have a clean people, a people that will stand for the whole counsel of God. Praise God for a people that are willing to stand for the Gospel and die for it if need be.

Ten

EVERYWHERE PREACHING THE WORD, SEPTEMBER 1907

THE APOSTOLIC FAITH

"Earnestly contend for the faith which was once delivered unto the saints."—Jude 3

Vol. 1, No. 10, Los Angeles, Cal., September, 1907, Subscription Free

This is a time as never before when the baptized saints are scattering abroad everywhere preaching the Word. They have gone out from Los Angeles far and near, carrying the sweet message that the Comforter has come. Some have gone to Canada, some east, some south, and some are on the way to foreign fields.

Many of the campmeeting saints are gathering back to the old "manger home" at Azusa. The pillar of fire still rests there. Meetings went on here all summer, souls seeking and finding the Lord.

The Lord taught His people at the Campground and gave them some practical experiences that will stand them in good stead on the field. The enemy came in as an angel of light, and we had a battle with the powers of darkness; but it was turned into victory after all. The Spirit was poured out and many souls baptized. God only knows the number. They were slain about the altars and in the "upper room tent," and came through speaking and singing in tongues and rejoicing in God.

Many were saved and sanctified. Over 100 were baptized in the stream near by. The baptizmal were sweet and heavenly. Numbers of children followed Jesus in baptism, and came out of the water praising God. Many testified to healing. The Lord performed some real miracles. Praise God!

There were over 200 living tents in the camp, besides a number of large tents; the big tabernacle where God met with us graciously; the "upper room tent" where many sought and obtained the

Pentecost; the children's tabernacle where they were taught the Word and many of them found the Lord, and we shall never forget that spot for it was so sweet to hear the children praying and praising the Lord; then there was the dining tent, where hundreds sat down to the tables and no charge made except as the Lord laid in on them to put into the box. We enjoyed some blessed times in the Spirit there, and also in the workers' dining tent, before we got the big tabernacle on the "all things common" line. One morning while at prayer after breakfast, the power of God so came on us that ten of the workers were slain and we did not get away till noon. We had a foretaste of heaven.

The hills around would sometimes ring with prayer and praise. Some sought and found the Lord on the hills, and came down with faces shining.

The early morning meetings before breakfast when all the saints met will never be forgotten. The Lord met with us. There were three other services

in the big tabernacle during the day, which often ran into the night, if not till morning. The altar workers were very faithful. They would stay and pray with seekers all night.

People came from hundreds and thousands of miles seeking Pentecost, and went back with the rivers of salvation. The songs from the camp could be heard distinctly up in Hermon. One sister who had been told it was all the power of the devil was up in Hermon listening, and she said to herself, "So that is the devil; well, the devil has some sweet singers." She came down and the result was she went to the altar and received the baptism with the Holy Ghost.

From Hermon, one sister saw fire issuing out of the tabernacle, as it were a tongue of fire. Her daughter also saw it. And a little boy who was in the power of the Spirit in the tabernacle, saw a ball of fire in the top of the tabernacle which broke and filled the whole place with light. God surely did send the fire. Many were the heavenly anthems the Spirit sang through His people. And He gave many beautiful messages in unknown tongues, speaking of His soon coming, invitations to come to the Lord, and exhortations from the Word.

We had some precious saints' meetings feasting on the Word. One blessed thing was the unity of the ministers and workers in the doctrines of the Bible, so plainly taught by our Lord. The Lord put His seal upon it. Those who were not present will find the doctrines in this paper as they were taught there. Our power in this Gospel is in standing in the Word. O how precious it is when we are in the Apostles' doctrine and fellowship. Some, it is sad to say, will not pay the price.

IN WASHINGTON, D. C.

In the capital city, the Pentecost has fallen in a colored Holiness Mission. Bro. and Sister S. S. Crawford were preaching the Pentecost at another mission, and they sent for them, as Cornelius sent for Peter to preach this Gospel. Twenty-two came to the altar the first service and four received Pentecost with the Bible evidence. The meeting went on for five weeks with 16 receiving the Pentecost, four of them preachers.

MINNESOTA CAMPMEETINGS

He is pouring out His Spirit on him that is thirsty and floods upon the dry ground. Our annual campmeeting at Fairmont Minn., June 14–24 was a season of precious waiting before the Lord. Heretofore it has been a tarrying place where the full Gospel was preached. But this year in the added light of Pentecostal blessings and power which a number present had received during the past few months, it swung out into a Pentecostal meeting. God was pleased to work graciously in our midst saving, sanctifying, and healing persons and several were baptized with the Holy Ghost, while the blessings flowed out upon others as the Holy Spirit fell upon the people.

At the Maxwell Campmeeting, on Thursday, July 5th, the Lord poured out His

Spirit in power; and while numbers were prostrate under the power, He was pleased to use two young women under the power of the Spirit, in speaking through them so that the hearts of the people were melted like wax in His presence, and realized they were in the very presence of God. The afternoon meeting merged into the evening meeting with no time to prepare supper. O it was most blessed indeed. —H. L. Blake, Ruthton, Minn.

IN NORTH CAROLINA

The Holy Ghost is being poured out in Rowan Free Will Baptist Church and many are speaking and singing in new tongues, and some interpreting and receiving other manifestations of the Spirit. On the 17th of May Bro. Harrell received his Pentecost, and from that time to this the Holy Ghost has been sought by others and about 28 have received their Pentecost, while several have been converted and some sanctified. In nearly every service someone gets their Pentecost. People are coming from other sections of the country to see for themselves the wonderful works of God in our midst.

The fire is falling at the F. W. Baptist Church at Frenches Creek, and also at the F. W. Baptist Church in Wilmington, N. C., and several have received their Pentecost at each of these places. At Wilmington there little girls from 10 to 12 years old have received their Pentecost and are gloriously happy. —A. J. Bordeau, Colly, N. C.

At High Point, N. C., the Pentecost mission is growing, souls are getting saved and the sick healed. At Durham, there is a happy band of baptized believers. At Winston-Salem, some are being baptized with the Holy Ghost and speaking in tongues.

IN NEW ORLEANS, LA.

As soon as we received those "Apostolic Faith" papers, we began praying, and fasted and prayed, and Glory to His name, He made Himself known in our midst, and came and baptized four with the Holy Ghost and fire. O what a grand time we did have, and the Lord has been continuing to baptize different ones. The fire is falling down here, and the Lord is bringing His saints together as Jesus prayed in the 17th of John. He is giving the gift of speaking with tongues and other gifts.—Alice Taylor, 2323 Washington Avenue

OTHER POINTS

In Oakland just as the paper goes to press, word comes from Sister Crawford who is on her way east that the power of God is falling. In San Francisco the work is going forward with two young brothers from the campmeeting in charge.

In Atlanta, Ga., reports come of many baptized with the Holy Ghost. Signs and wonders have been given by the Lord.

At Dayton, Ohio, the Holy Ghost first fell in February on those that were earnestly seeking the fullness. Thirty-six souls were reported to have received the Pentecost and the altar full of seekers. Bro. W. W. Bailey, a baptized preacher there opened up a Pentecost Gospel Union Mission at 767 S. Brown St.

At Chambersburg, Pa., about 25 got baptized and some spoke in tongues, some saved, sanctified and healed.

At Youngstown, Ohio, a number have received the baptism. One night they were in prayer all the evening praising God and the Lord gave the heavenly song which sounded to them like angelic strains. One sister saw into glory and saw the heavenly city. Such a sight to behold! It seemed the celestial city was so near, the veil was almost worn through.

At Memphis, Tenn., many hungry souls have been baptized.

At Durant, Fla., there has been a gracious meeting in which about 50 have received the Holy Ghost. Some have been healed, unclean spirits crying with loud voices have come out of some that were possessed with them, souls are saved and sanctified.

Pentecost has fallen at Council Bluffs Ia., at Caldwell, Kans., at Mankato, Minn. at New Castle, Pa., at Watertown, N. Y., and the work has been increasing at many other points.

Truly this is a refreshing time, according to Acts 3:18–21. "Repent ye therefore and be converted, that your sins may be blotted out, when the time of refreshing shall come from the presence of the Lord. And He shall send Jesus Christ." We can see the refreshing times are now flowing.

In Portland, Oregon, there has been a Holy Ghost camp-meeting going on all summer. Hundreds have been baptized with the Holy Ghost, many saved, sanctified and healed. They have such love and harmony among the saints that they have all things on Pentecostal lines. The saints there are mostly poor, yet making many rich. Tents and eating tabernacle free and no collections. God abundantly supplied. Portland has become an example of this Pentecostal faith. Glory to God for what He has done.

This great movement is like a little mustard seed planted in Los Angeles. It took root in a humble place which proved to be good soil and, watered with

rivers from heaven, it soon put forth its branches to nearby towns as Long Beach and out to Oakland. Soon the limbs spread north and far over the eastern states, and then clear over into Sweden and India. Now it is spreading all over the world, and how beautiful and green it is, and how the birds are coming to lodge in its branches.

Christ is making up His jewels quickly. O how the "latter rain" is falling. We hear from Canada, from the east and south the sound of abundance of rain. Praise God. It is falling in Sweden, in Norway and refreshing showers in India. Also we hear of gracious drops falling in other distant lands. We hear the rumbling of the chariots of heaven. Some are trying to stop it but you might as well try to stop a cloud burst in the mountains. This thing is in God's hands.

Men and women have prayed for years to see this precious light, prayed to see Los Angeles revived. Now we can see the fruits of Pentecost here, God healing people, saving, sanctifying, baptizing with the Holy Ghost, speaking through the power of the Spirit and singing in unknown tongues, giving sweet anthems from heaven. God has graciously answered the prayers of His people, though many are blinded and cannot see it; but praise God, our eyes have seen this great salvation and we ought to be encouraged to go forward as never before.

In Minneapolis there is a precious Holy Ghost mission band of about 200 Holy Ghost people who are united in love and harmony, filled with the glory of God. Though they have been persecuted and maligned by the secular papers, yet God has only used it as free advertisement to draw honest souls. One woman heard of it 250 miles away and came all the way to receive her Pentecost, and in a short time she received a mighty baptism with the Holy Ghost, speaking in tongues and interpreting, and

went back with the precious oil of the Holy Ghost.

Hungry souls rejoice to hear of the Pentecost. Sister Mary Yaegge of Baltimore was one who rejoiced to hear of the Pentecost at Los Angeles. She prized the little paper for it seemed to be just what her soul longed for. She had been raised a Catholic and had received the Gospel gladly and was sanctified and hungering for the Holy Ghost. She came to the campmeeting. Received her Pentecost on the way, while at Oakland and is truly anointed with power and divine love. She is on her way back to Switzerland, her native home, to give this Gospel to her people.

Missionaries in China have been seeking the baptism with the Holy Ghost ever since they received the first "Apostolic Faith" papers from Los Angeles. One dear missionary, Brother B. Berntsen from South Chih-li, Tai-Ming-Fu, North China, came all the way to Los Angeles to receive his Pentecost. And, bless God, he went to the altar at Azusa Mission, and soon fell under the power, and arose drunk on the new wine of the kingdom, magnifying God in a new tongue. As soon as he could speak English, he said, "This means much for China." Then he told how he had felt the need of the fullness of the Pentecost in China, and we fell on our knees and prayed that the dear missionaries might be anointed and China might receive the Gospel.

The manager of the Union Rescue Mission in Los Angeles, Bro. Will Trotter, received the baptism with the Holy Ghost and as a result he lost his position under men, but God has marvelously anointed him and is using him in the evangelistic work.

In Chicago there are a number of Pentecostal meetings. Many are magnifying God for the baptism with the Holy Ghost. The Lord is using Bro.

Durham as a river that overflows its banks and waters the thirsty ground. Many hungry ones are seeking and obtaining their baptism. Some of the Moody Institute people have received their Pentecost, but the theologians are not accepting it.

The Scandinavian Apostolic Faith Mission at 775 Wall Street, Los Angeles, is one of the sweetest places you ever were in. The people there are filled with the Spirit praising God. They seem so sincere and full of divine love. There are a number of precious young men and women there that God has cleansed and filled with the Spirit. It is blessed to see them.

THE LOVE OF JESUS

"Surely He hath borne our griefs and carried our sorrows." The Son of God went into the garden when He was bearing this world of sin. The blood gushed out from His skin and fell in great drops to the ground. He prayed, "Father, if it be thy will remove this cup from me, nevertheless not my will but Thine be done." He suffered until His heart swelled in His body and forced the blood through the flesh. His soul burned in Him with the weight of sin of this old world on our conquering King. Then He did not stop but went through Pilate's judgement hall and was whipped and the blood ran down in that judgment hall, and was shed all the way to Calvary. O those stripes reach our sicknesses and our infirmities and heal us. He bled and died and went down into the grave and rose again. O beloved, He atoned for you. He hung and bled for you, and if you will accept Him today He will fill your heart.

At the Christian and Missionary Alliance Convention in Nyack, New York, some were present who had received their Pentecost, and a great interest was awakened. In a tarrying meeting one young lady who was called to Africa fell under the power, received the baptism with the Holy Ghost and began to speak in an African tongue, which was recognized by missionaries from Africa as being the very language of the part of Africa to which the sister was expecting to go. Others sought and obtained the baptism.

A minister who had been opposing this work went to one of the Pentecostal meetings and got under conviction. He confessed to all that he was in the wrong and stated to his congregation that he must have this Pentecostal power, that he would not preach until he had it; he would work on the rock pile first. Then he called all his people to the altar that wanted it and they came in crowds. O the hungry souls. If the ministers would only go in themselves and let their hungry flocks go in what a wave of salvation there would be. This minister we hear has been mightily baptized and many of his people.

In Santa Barbara in a Pentecostal meeting, as they were kneeling about the altar, some whiskey bottles were thrown which came from a saloon near by. Two of the saints were struck with them. Sister Crawford was cut on the temple by one of these ugly weapons, but the saints prayed for her and the meeting went on. She writes that she is rejoicing to be counted worthy to bear about in her body the marks of the Lord Jesus.

In Zion City, Ill., a little girl of about six years came to her mother and said she was going to get saved. She went upstairs and commenced to pray, and the Lord heard her. She called down to her mother "Mamma, if something in me says I am saved, is that Jesus?" Her mother said, "Yes." Again she prayed and called to her mother, "Mamma, if something in me says I am sanctified, is that Jesus speaking?" Her mother said, "Yes." Then she said, "Mamma, I am sanctified." She got down and prayed again and was baptized with the Holy Ghost, and the Lord has had her preaching, and gave her a message

to one of Dowie's elders that had fought this work. So God spoke through this little child unable to read. He could preach through the ass of Balaam and He can take a little child and preach through it.

We must keep where God can use us, and the secret is humility, the Word and the Blood.

This Gospel, the full Gospel of Jesus must be preached in all the earth for a witness then shall the end come.

Jesus Christ tasted death for every man but He did not taste death for the devil or fallen angels. We do not believe the devil or fallen angels are going to be saved. The Lord Jesus did not die for the devil or demons. Everyone that will repent of their sins can find rest in the Blood of Calvary.

When Christ is in you, He is married to you in spirit. He calls you, "My love and My dove." Everyone that has Christ is married to Him in spirit. "Ye are become dead to the law by the body of Christ; that ye should be married to another, even to Him who is raised from the dead." Rom. 7:4. We are under the law of the Spirit of Christ. O how sweet it is. You would not depart from this husband of your soul for anything.

Eleven

Good Tidings of Great Joy, January 1908

The Apostolic Faith

"Earnestly contend for the faith which was once delivered unto the saints."—Jude 3

Vol. 1, No. 11, Los Angeles, Cal., October to January, 1908, Subscription Free

Pentecost in Many Lands—News of Salvation—Jesus Soon Coming

Pentecost Spreads to Other Lands

Denmark

"Kirkekiokken," a Danish gospel paper, reports that through the Copenhagen Pentecostal outburst recently, many sinners have come to the Savior, many backsliders have been restored to the joy of salvation, many believers have been filled with the Spirit and have received supernatural gifts.

In Wales

"Praise God for another brother here who has also now received the Pentecost with tongues. He went home from here speaking in tongues all along the street. There are others to follow. Glory to Jesus. Tonight five or six brothers are coming here for their Pentecost. O, I do praise God that He sent me to Sunderland to get such a wonderful blessing. Praise His holy name."—W. J. Tomlinson, Lynton House, Grove Place, Port Talbot

Honolulu

Brother and Sister Turney, who have returned from Honolulu, now on their way to Africa report the work in Honolulu: "We had a glorious meeting Honolulu. The power came down and one young man a captain of the Salvation Army, who received his Pentecost, has now opened up an Apostolic Faith Mission in Santa Cruz, Cal. A lieutenant also received his Pentecost and went to carry the news to London, England. Charley Puck, who had a most wonderful experience, is preaching the Gospel on the Island of Hawaii in the city of Kanuela. They are

143

having good meetings and good attendance. People are hungry for the truth.

LONDON, ENGLAND

I do thank God that there are a few whose eyes God has opened to see their lack and who have waited upon His in prayer for quite a year and a half at 14 Ackerman Rd., Brixon S. W., London. God has manifested His almighty power there in the baptism of dear Sister Price and one brother and myself, and I am so glad to send in my testimony to the glory of God and the encouragement of all His children. People are coming from far and near, and no one has even been invited. They just hear how God is working and come. This power was mightily present last Thursday, two sisters being shaken and nearly spoke in tongues. One night the very room was shaken as we read in the Word: "And when they had prayed the place was shaken." Several have had blessed anointings, outpourings of the Spirit and revelations of Jesus Christ. Praise His Holy name.

—Mary A. Martin, 319 Southampton St., Camberwell, London, England

CHINA

Brother and Sister Garr are in Hong Kong, China, last report. God is using them blessedly. A glorious revival is breaking out. Several souls in Hong Kong have received their Pentecost.

In Macao and Canton, China, numbers have received the baptism with the Spirit. They are hungry for the Holy Ghost. Brother McIntosh wrote, "They come to our house at all times of the day and rap at our door at 11 and 12 o'clock at night, coming to seek for the Holy Ghost, and we stay up till one and two o'clock praying with them, and glory to God, the Pentecost falls and they speak in tongues." Two sisters who received their Pentecost in Brother Cashwell's work in the South have gone over to help Brother and Sister McIntosh. They are Sister A. E. Kirby and Sister Mabel Evans. Address Macao, China, care S. C. Todd.

SWEDEN

Bramaregarden, Hisingstad, Goteborg, Nov. 19.—"I am very glad to hear from the old Azusa Mission, my home. I have victory through the dear, cleansing Blood of Christ. Glory to His great name! It is one year today since I came over to Sweden and this city Goteborg. God is still saving, sanctifying, and baptizing with the Holy Ghost, and people are getting healed of God. Last Sunday two got their Pentecostal blessing. We had a wonderful day, the Holy Ghost running the meetings, God's children testifying, praising God, talking in unknown tongues. The fire has begun to fall on small islands near the city. Bless God! The work is still going on in many places in Sweden and God's people are getting more hungry than ever. We trust God to send out more workers in the field. The fire is falling in 'Norrland.' Yet many, many have not heard this Gospel yet. This work will go on till Jesus our Lord comes back. All the saints in Goteborg salute you."—Andrew G. Johnson

GERMANY

"Auf der Warte," a German paper, says:

At Cassel many children of God received the fullness of the Spirit after God had cleansed their hearts by faith. Many children of God have put right old debts. Through the speaking in tongues and the preaching, sins and bonds were revealed, and it was clearly taught that deliverance from the power of sin and the experience of heart cleansing are the conditions for receiving the Pentecostal baptism.

The manifestations of the Spirit when the souls were touched were different according to I Cor. 12. Some were knocked down to the floor, some were overflowed gently while sitting in their chairs. Some cried with a loud voice, others shouted Hallelujah! clapped their hands, jumped or laughed with joy. Some saw the Lord not only in the meetings, but when silent in the houses, or in bed, or when walking on the road, God touched their souls.

All that was uttered in

tongues as far as it concerned salvation was in perfect accord with Scripture. What the Lord gave to utter about His Cross, His Glory, and the Second Coming was refreshment and comfort for every believing soul. Through the speaking of tongues and prophesy those in the audience received conviction of their sins; which statement is proven by confessions made afterwards to the minister.

The fire is already burning at Grossalmerode. The Lord is doing great things. Many have received the Pentecostal baptism; and the Lord bestowed gifts upon many, especially the gift of tongues and interpretation.

WITNESSES IN ENGLAND
(FROM REPORTS PRINTED AT SUNDERLAND, ENG.)
CHILDREN RECEIVE PENTECOST

I was present when the two girls, who were the first children to speak in tongues in England, Janie and May Boddy (the two daughters of the Rev. Alex. A. Boddy, All Saints' Vicarage, Sunderland), received their Pentecost. It was at the Vicarage.

The nine or ten persons present will never forget the scene. Janie received the interpretation for each sentence, and her childlike simplicity and joy, her beaming face, that I shall never forget, she turned message she received was: "Jesus is coming!" With a surprised look of joy on her face, that I shall never forget, she turned to her mother and kissed her, repeating the words: "Jesus is coming, mother!"

Then her face became serious. She bowed her head a little and lifted her left hand to her cheek (she was kneeling all the time at the end of the table). Again a foreign language was heard. Then came the interpretation: "The Heavens are opened!" followed by the same jubilant glee.

One message was very solemn, spoken, too, with emphasis: "The first shall be last, and the last first." Coming from such childlike lips, it made a great impression on us all.

Oh, what joy when she said: "Oh! Mummie, Jesus has come, and come to stay; oh, good Jesus, good Jesus!" then peals of joybells of laughter.

As she related her experience the next day to a large crowd of children at the Parish Hall, she said, whilst inviting them to seek their Pentecost, "Oh, it is so wonderful, so wonderful!" It was wonderful, it was the Holy Spirit come to dwell within them.

May Boddy had a great revelation of God's power. She prayed so earnestly that she might not "be left out." It was touching, too, to see Janie, who had just received her Pentecost, as she laid her hand on her sister's head and encouraged her: "It's all through the Blood, May, all through the Blood! Jesus is come, He said. May too, May too."

May spoke a long time. Some words were quite clear. It seemed as if she was constantly claiming Jesus. His name was repeated time upon time. The words, "Aa, Ja, Jesus! Ja, ja, ja, Jesus!" were distinctly Norwegian, with the correct pronunciation (Oh yes, Jesus! yes, yes, Jesus!)

These two dear children have been kind and good girls before and loved Jesus dearly but now they love Him much more and are bold to tell others of His wonderful power to save.—T. B. Barratt

TESTIMONY OF A VICAR'S WIFE

After a long time of silent waiting upon Him, God gave me a wonderful vision of Christ in the glory at the right hand of the Father, and from Him came a wonderful light on me, causing me to laugh as I had never done before. I thought this was the Baptism, for this gave me more power in speaking for Christ, and more realization of His indwelling, but yet God has a more excellent way for me. After waiting with others for months at home, in eager and earnest expectation of His Baptism of Fire, God chose that when the fire did begin to fall here, I should be in the South of England, not able to return for nearly a fortnight, and several had received their Pentecost. God was working in me more than I realized, literally drying up all experience, all spiritual life of the flesh. When I returned home on the evening of the 10th of September, I felt utterly callous, and even, to my surprise, uninterested. I could not pray, nor read, nor even think of God, but just rested by naked faith on the Word of God that "I was dead," and only Christ was my all-in-all.

I went to the meeting the next evening, but could not sing nor pray, I just rested in God and asked Him to lead the Pastor to lay hands on me when He wished. Soon the Pastor was "filled with the Holy Ghost" and came to me. When he laid hands on me, I expected a great rush of feeling, such as I have often experienced, as the Life of Jesus thrilled through my body, but I felt nothing. The Spirit then flashed light on to the Word, "They laid hands on them and they received the Holy Ghost." I should like to emphasize that it was at this point of really believing in my heart God's Word, that I had received

(Acts viii., 17), that He began to manifest His presence (the empty, cleansed vessel receiving the outpoured gift), and I just rested again in the fact that God the Holy Ghost had come and would do His own work. Suddenly the Lord filled His Temple and I was in the glory. What followed I cannot describe, and it is too sacred to do so, but I knew God had come. Though never unconscious, I was quite oblivious to everyone around, just worshipping. Then my mouth began to quiver, my tongue began to move, and a few simple words were uttered, as I just yielded to the Holy Ghost. Much to my astonishment, I began to speak fluently in a foreign language—Chinese I think. The Spirit sang through me. The joy and rapture of this purely spiritual worship can never be described. If for no other purpose, I felt at last satisfied that "there was no difference between me and them as at the bginning," Acts xi., 15. Then came a vision of the Blood. As the Spirit spoke that word I was conscious that

ALL heaven, oh glory! (myself included) was "worshipping the Lamb, as it had been slain." Oh, the efficacy, the power of the Blood. In one moment, what I had believed in for years was illuminated as a reality. Nothing else can take its place, it is the Blood that cleanseth. Then came more words in 'tongues' with the interpretation. "Worthy is thre Lamb; Jesus is coming."

People say, "What is the difference now?" Just this, and this is all the difference. What one has held on to by faith in the Word, is a reality. I know, as never before, that Christ liveth in me. The Power to love and believe and witness is there, as never before; and last, though not least, after longing with a hungry heart for years to satisfy my God and Saviour, that "He might see the travail of His soul and be satisfied," I thank Him with all my heart that at last He has received from me pure spirit-worship— "mysteries,"—1 Cor. 14, 2; John 3, 23. I recognize, as never before, that it is still a walk of faith and obedience, that I am nothing and Christ is my all in all. I am launched out into the fathomless ocean of God's love, joy and peace. It is "joy unspeakable and full of glory." I thank God for the Pentecostal sign of 'tongues.' I did not ask for 'tongues' but for the Holy Ghost, and He "gave me utterance," and the joy of praising God in the Spirit is truly wonderful.—Mrs. A. A. Body, Sunderland, Eng.

TESTIMONY OF A SUNDAY SCHOOL TEACHER

On Sunday, September 8th, I surrendered my whole being fully to Jesus and accepted cleansing through His most precious Blood, and on Monday, September 9th, while reading a little booklet, I got a great blessing from these two verses:

Nothing to settle? all has
    been paid,
Nothing of anger? peace
    has been made;
Jesus alone is the sinner's
    resource
Peace He has made by the
    Blood of His cross.
Nothing of guilt? no, not
    a stain,

How could the Blood let any remain,

My conscience is purged, my spirit is free, Precious that Blood is to God and to me.

And then I claimed my Pentecost through that precious Blood, and stood firm on the blessed promises in Luke xi., 13, and Luke xxiv., 49, and I praised Him for it until Friday, September 13th. Oh, that glorious night when Christ came into my heart in all His fulness. It was about twenty minutes to nine when I went into the meeting and they were singing "Rest in the Lord," the message He gave me on Thursday, Psalm xxxvii., 7. A dear sister gave me the card with "Now I give up all to Jesus" on, and told me to let all go and just yield to Him, and oh, the unspeakable joy that flooded my soul when I, in simple faith, let my whole heart go. It was Jesus Himself who came in, glory to His Name. I could have shouted Glory, Hallelujah! all the way home. On Sunday, September 15th, we had a prayer meeting at a friend's house and the Spirit fell mightily upon me and I spoke in a strange language. Oh, it's all Glory, Glory, Glory, I cannot explain the joy and peace I now have, but I know it is all through the precious Blood of Jesus. Praise Him, praise Him.

TESTIMONY OF A YORKSHIRE FARMER

The Holy Spirit came upon me on Sunday night, showing me the mighty power in the blood of Jesus. The following night it was Jesus himself and the Holy Spirit entering in like a flood. I do thank the Lord that He enabled me to take Him in, or rather, He so melted me that I allowed Him to come in. I took Him in all His fulness, that the life of the head might be the life of the member of the body. How unnatural it would seem to see a person going around within the head and not the same life running through the body and the head no control over the body. I feel that I want to be like the bed of a river, perfectly still, but wide enough to admit a flood.

When I got home on Tuesday night, I was sitting by myself occupied with the Lord, when I got the sign of tongues. Glory to the name of Jesus.

PENTECOSTAL MISSIONARY REPORTS

Since the last paper, Spirit-filled missionaries have gone out from Los Angeles to Monrovia, Liberia, Africa, two sisters to South China and a band of nine missionaries to North China. Also a band of fourteen missionaries went from Spokane, Wash., to Japan and China. They were able to talk to the Chinese and Japanese at the dock and on the ship in their native language. The "Apostolic Light" is now published by Brother Ryan in Tokyo, Japan.

Our dear Brother A. H. Post who is on his way to South Africa from Los Angeles, writes from London, England, "Praise our God, the 'latter rain' is falling in England. Glory to our God forever. I do greatly rejoice in Him for this blessed privilege of carrying this wonderful salvation to other nations. My heart leaps with joy and burns with His love for so great a privilege." Address him at 14 Ackeranm Road, Brixton, London, S. W., care Mrs. Price.

We never saw a more humble and Spirit-filled band of missionaries than the dear ones that left Los Angeles for North China, going by the way of Seattle where they were joined by others, making twelve in all, besides children. Brother Bernsten, Brother and Sister Hess and six workers from the Swedish Mission, made up the company from here. They went out trusting God alone for their support. Brother Bernsten says, "God has laid it on my heart to go to a new field and open up the work there. It is on the railroad line south of Peking, a big field, and to open our home for any independent worker filled with the Holy Ghost and fire, to come and stay with us until they are sure where God wants them. Pray for a dwelling-place and a home convenient for Chinese orphans." We are expecting God to wonderfully bless these consecrated and anointed ones. They are going into the famine district.—B. Bernsten, Taiming fu, Chihli, North China

-----

Our dear Sister Farrow, who was one of the first to bring Pentecost to Los Angeles, went to Africa and spent seven months at Johnsonville, 25 miles from Monrovia, Liberia, in that most deadly climate. She has now returned and has a wonderful story to tell. Twenty souls received their Pentecost, numbers were saved sanctified and healed. The Lord had given her the gift of the Kru language and she was permitted to preach two sermons to the people in their own tongue. The heathen some of them after receiving the Pentecost, spoke in English and some in other tongues. Praise God. The Lord showed her when she went, the time she was to return and sent her the fare in time, brought her home safely, and used her in Virginia and in the South along the way.

There is no man at the head of this movement. God Himself is speaking in the earth. We are on the verge of the greatest miracle the world has ever seen, when the sons of God shall be manifested, the saints shall come singing from the dust (Isa. 26:19) and the full overcomers shall be caught up to meet the Lord in the air. The political world realizes that some great crisis is at hand, the scientific world, the religious world all feel it. The coming of the Lord draweth night, it is near, even at the doors.

Twelve

THE LORD IS SPEAKING IN THE EARTH TODAY, JANUARY 1908

THE APOSTOLIC FAITH

"Earnestly contend for the faith which was once delivered unto the saints."—Jude 3

Vol. 1, No. 12, Los Angeles, Cal., January, 1908, Subscription Free

Indianapolis, Ind.—Many souls have been baptized in Indianapolis, saved and sanctified.

Norwood, Ohio.—Our people are growing, fourteen baptized and interest increasing.—W. H. Cossum, 3952 Hazel Avenue

Colly, N. C.—The fire is still burning here in our midst and souls are being converted and sanctified and baptized with the Holy Ghost.—A. J. Bordeau

Atlanta, Ga.—The meetings in the hall here have been blessed seasons of refreshing. For six months, every afternoon and night and all day on Sundays, the meetings have continued. Before this "latter rain" such revivals were unheard of. Souls are being saved, sanctified, and healed, and filled with the Holy Ghost. All glory to Jesus' name! Let us follow on to know Him better. This is the beginning of great things.—"The Bridegroom's Messenger," 53½ Auburn Avenue

Hill River. Minn.—I am thankful to God for what He has done for a small group of Christians here in the town of Hill River, where I live. Quite a few have received their Pentecost and others seeking it, and we are continuing to pray to God for His blessing in a greater degree.—Andrew Hausan, Fosston, Minn.

Utica, N. Y.—Blessed be the name of the Lord. Truly these days of the "latter rain" are days of Heaven upon the earth. We are a little band here but full of faith and pressing on. One by one, God is bringing our number into their Pentecost, and is opening other places where there are a few hungry believers longing for their inheritance.—Birdsell & Mason,

61 State Street
Concord Junction, Mass.—
God is working in this place.
Five of us have the baptism,
speaking in tongues and others
getting hungry. He came in
to abide with me on Oct.
16th and spoke for Himself.
—Everett E. Munroe, 397
Main Street

Strole, Va.—Pentecost has
come here. Eight of us are
speaking in tongues. Thieves,
gamblers and drunkards
have been saved. Praise the
dear Lord. We are looking
for dear Jesus every day and
can hardly wait to see Him.
—W. S. Woodworth, Caanan
Faith Home and Full Gospel
Mission

Portsmouth and Richmond,
Va.—Brother Seymour wrote
from these places while he was
visiting the missions in the
East: "God is working in Portsmouth. Souls were baptized in
Richmond and God is working
in mighty power. The saints
are just as sweet as can be.
Glory to God for this Gospel.
The saints are so simple here,
that is the reason they receive
the Pentecost so quickly. They

are ready for the power."

Philadelphia, Pa.—I have
been helping in the Pentecostal work in one little meeting here. There were a number
at the altar last Sunday and
a number were slain under
the mighty power of God.
I had a letter from a sister in
Danville, Va., a few days ago,
and she says that God is blessing them there and that souls
are being saved, sanctified,
and baptized with the Holy
Ghost. Hallelujah! Hallelujah!
—W. M. Scott, 906 Filbert
Street, Dec. 4

Swanton, Ohio. —Praise
the Lord. A few have been
baptized near home here and
a great many more are hungry
for more of God. We have had
a few wonderful conventions
here in Ohio the past summer.
One of the most wonderful
meetings was at the Annual
Christian Alliance Convention
at Cleveland. Some evenings
there were perhaps from three
to four hundred down at the
altar, some remaining all night;
and a great many received
their baptism, and many were
saved. Praise the Lord. Jesus

is certainly soon coming!
—Gideon Ziegler

Baltimore, Ohio.—There is a little mission here where the leader and about ten people had been seeking for their baptism for seven months, but none of them came through until last night, when the leader came through gloriously and others have been under the power and some sanctified. Praise God!—Mary A. Yaegge, 1022 N. Eutaw Street. (This sister is on her way to Switzerland, where the Lord is calling her to preach the Gospel.)

Denver, Colo.—Our meetings are being blessed of God. Souls are being saved, sanctified, baptized with the Holy Ghost and healed, and the interest is still increasing. All glory be to God for His wonderful works that He is bestowing upon His children, as He is pouring out His Spirit upon all flesh in these latter days: for the coming of the Lord draweth nigh. The Lord has held us here and He has opened up an Apostolic Faith Mission on the corner of Lawrence and Twenty-fourth Streets.

The altar is filled with seekers.
—E. S. Lee, 2305 Lawrence Street

Lynn, Mass.—We are now holding meetings in the mission at 260 Maple Street. We commenced this work in a hall last February. One of our number, a girl born blind and blind for twenty-two years, healed and sanctified about eight years ago, received her personal Pentecost last March. She speaks, sings and preaches in different languages, has visions and prophecy. The Lord showed her this mission about two months before we had it. The Lord gave us the name of the mission, Apostolic Faith Mission. A number have been saved and sanctified, speak in new tongues and a number have been healed.
—A. J. Rawson, Oct. 26th

Dallas, Ore.—In the camp-meeting here last summer about thirty were baptized with the Holy Spirit, with the evidence of speaking in tongues as the Spirit gave utterance. Many were saved and sanctified. Brother Earnest G. Hansen writes on Jan. 6th: "Since I last wrote, about eight backsliders have got back to the Lord, some have been sanctified, two have been baptized with the Holy Ghost. Meetings are grand." They have a precious little paper there, clean and straight in doctrines, called "The Apostolic Witness."

Portland, Ore.—At 224 Madison Street, they have a blessed Apostolic Faith Mission. The saints are filled and overflowing with the Spirit and with love for souls, talking and singing in tongues. The hall is not nearly large enough. Altars are filled with seekers. We shall never forget the precious visit we had there. One secret of the power here is the prayer room where the workers drop in for silent prayer before the services—not to talk or visit. Souls were being saved, sanctified, and baptized. A bartender got wonderfully saved of God, and when he rose and tried to tell it, he broke down and fell on his knees and began to thank Jesus, and it filled everyone with joy. We have lately received some precious letters from Portland telling of God's work there.

With the dear saints in New York. God is working there. Many are coming through. In one church—a Baptist colored church of two thousand members—God used us to give out these "latter rain" truths. The pastor who invited us became very hungry. He said he could not preach again till he was filled. Seven from his church received the promise of the Father, Acts 2: 4. Hallelujah to Jesus! Went down to Norfolk, Va., and found quit a few baptized souls. God sent us up here to Baltimore and we found a little assembly here of baptized souls. We are out for God and wherever the Lamb goeth, we intend to follow. —Brother and Sister E. W. Vinton, 12 Leyden Street, Medford, Mass.

Chicago, Ill.—God is wonderfully working here. Both the interest and power are increasing. We have stood by the simple Gospel here from the very first, preaching only Jesus Christ and Him crucified. And as we have done this, the Holy Ghost has fallen on them that heard the Word, so that tongue can never tell what we have experienced. Praise the Lord!—Wm. H. Durham, 943 W. North Avenue

Sister Jennie E. Moore, who with two other precious sisters from Azusa Mission, Los Angeles, have been working in Chicago and other places, writes: "Truly, beloved, the mission at 943 W. North Avenue is a blessed place—many Spirit-filled men and women and children. They have more children than at Azusa and they are filled. Beloved, I wish you could see them."

Winnipeg, Can.—There was a great Pentecostal Convention in Winnipeg beginning November 15th. Preachers and workers from all parts of Canada were present. A band of workers who were in Portland at the time received a call from God to go to Winnipeg, and they were present at the convention: Sister Crawford and Mildred, Sister Neal, Brother Conlee and Brother Trotter. About twenty were baptized with the Holy Ghost and many were healed. The people brought handkerchiefs and aprons to be blessed as in Acts 19: 12, and the Lord did wonderful signs through the simple faith of the dear ones that brought them. The Lord healed one young man of the tobacco habit, taking all the desire away from him, through an anointed handkerchief, and he was saved in his own room. Demons were cast out of those bound by them. Our last published report from Winnipeg should have been signed, "The Apostolic Faith Mission, 501 Alexander Ave.,"

Arcadia, Fla., and through the South.—Brother G. B. Cashwell and I are in the midst of a gracious revival in this town. The power is falling and saints are shouting. Bless God! Some have been saved, sanctified, and quite a number have received the Holy Ghost and speaking with other tongues as the Spirit gives utterance as in Acts 2: 4. The altar is filled with seekers. God has kept me in Florida most all this year. Many saints have received the Holy Ghost in Florida with Bible evidence and many saved. A number of them have been baptized in water, buried in baptism, that is the Bible way.—F. M. Britton, Dec. 11.

Brother Cashwell writes from the South: "This truth in the South is spreading as never before and will keep spreading as Praise our God! Pray much and be true to Jesus. Many of us are now suffering much persecution, but our God is fighting our battles. Praise His dear name! Brother McIntosh writes me that seventy have received the Holy Ghost in thirty days after he arrived in Macao, China. O praise God for Pentecost. Salute all the saints for me in the love of Jesus!"—G. B. Cashwell, 53½ Auburn Avenue, Atlanta, Ga.

Stockton, Cal.—Five or six have been baptized with the Holy Ghost and several saved and several cases of healing.

Shenandoah, Iowa. —"Salvation has come. Hallelujah! God has come our way at last. Amen. Last Friday afternoon at Francis Jones' a few of us were gathered pleading for the baptism of the Holy Spirit and He gave us the desire of our hearts at last. Glory , O glory. Two of us received our baptism, Sister Leyden and I. The rest are hard after Him. They were here at our house until after three this morning. There is quite a company of us. Sister Leyden lay under the power for several hours and talked and sang in the Spirit and the Lord let me join in the song and sing too. Glory, glory, hallelujah! Blessed be the name of Jesus. The song was "Worthy is the Lamb", and nearly the whole chapter. She interpreted it afterwards." —Sister J. S. Jellison

Minneapolis and St. Paul, Minn. —Wonderful outpouring of the Spirit here and at St. Paul. In five nights just passed in St. Paul alone, nine have received old time baptisms of the Holy Ghost and fire, speaking in many dialects and receiving wonderful visions from the Lord. Amen! Nine have been blessedly sanctified. One woman dying with cancer—given up to die by three specialists, next morning after being prayed for arose and did her work, and has been doing it ever since—healed. I was in St. Paul last week and Brother Trotter was here, and in both places, the power was wonderful—yesterday especially, many being instantly healed and many saved. People were prostrated under the power of God at 11:30 last night. Many were heavily anointed for their baptism, and we expect a shower in the next few days. Glory is abiding in our hearts. —Florence Crawford, 1315 East 19th Street, Minneapolis, Minn., Jan. 6.

A later report written Jan. 13th, says: "I wish to report victory in both St. Paul and Minneapolis. Yesterday was a great day. We had the ordinances of the Lord's Supper and Foot-Washing Saturday night, and saints from St. Paul all came over and participated with us. Some fell under the power and lay for several hours. We had a blessed time. We then invited St. Paul saints to worship with us on Sunday afternoon. Sister Crawford gave the message in the after-

noon. I gave it in the morning; and Brother Trotter in the evening. People fell under the power all day. And when I left the hall at 5 p.m., they were lying all over the hall under the power. The hall was an altar from the stand to the door. So many are getting saved, and many that have been claiming to be sanctified are finding that they were just saved, and are now getting really sanctified. Greetings to the church at Azusa Street." —J. R. Conlee, 1003 25th Avenue, N. E., Minneapolis

FROM AZUSA MISSION

Many souls have been saved, sanctified, baptized with the Holy Ghost and sick bodies healed all over the land and in many lands since our last paper. Souls have been sanctified, baptized and saved at the old mission home at 312 Azusa Street, Los Angeles.

When Christ was born, it was in a barn at Bethlehem; and when He began sending the "latter rain" about two years ago, the outpouring of the Spirit, it was in a barn in Los Angeles; for the old Mission is like a barn in its humility and plainness. Its old beams and whitewashed walls have been ringing with the praises and songs of the children of God ever since. Many from here have gone out into the foreign fields and the home fields, and they write back that they remember the blessed old times; and the Lord has been pouring out the same Spirit wherever He has sent them. The Spirit falls on humble hearts and in humble missions and churches.

Azusa Mission is still giving forth the same truth, and the Lord is pouring out His Spirit upon His sons and daughters, and they are witnessing in burning testimonies that Jesus' Blood does cleanse from all sin and He does sanctify and baptize with the Holy Ghost and speak in tongues.

The holidays are special feast days at the Mission. The saints all gather—not to hear a program, for the Holy Ghost makes the program and the Father spreads the table with "the fatted calf" which represents Jesus, and we feed on Christ. Hallelulah! The Spirit sings the songs, some new and some old. Christmas was a blessed day at the Mission, also Watch Night and New Year's Day. The meetings have been going on every day since the work started and God's word and the Holy Spirit are just as fresh and new as ever. The Lord provided for all the expenses. He has supplied all the needs of the workers, and when they come back they report that they have lacked for nothing.

The devil is doing all he can to keep the saints from entering into the greater fullness of Christ; but we know God is raising up armies that will stand for the living God. Some went away from Azusa Mission because they thought the teaching on divorce was too straight; but God will not let us lower the standard. He wants a clean people and pure doctrine as a channel for this Pentecostal power. People everywhere are looking after this wonderful salvation that today is turning the world upside down, as it did in Paul's time.

We look for a great outpouring of God's Spirit in saving and healing power and power that fills with the Holy Ghost and fire in this year 1908. May all Christ's people be stirred up over this salvation and sink down in deeper humility at the feet of Jesus.

"If we walk in the light as He is in the light, the Blood of Jesus Christ, His Son, cleanseth us from all sin." (I John 1, 7.) Bless His name forever and ever! It is the Blood that cleanseth, the precious Blood of Jesus. May we honor the Blood and keep under the Blood, and God will do mighty things for us. If the devil can get us on something outside of God, He will break our power. May we be watchful and keep under the Blood. The Lord wants the Blood preached as never before, and people will not have to wait so long to get the baptism. The Spirit follows the Blood. It is the Blood that saves us. We overcame by the Blood. Amen!

FROM THE BIBLE SCHOOL IN MUKTI, INDIA

It was noticed one day, that some of the girls in the praying band were praying in different tongues. I had heard of the gift of tongues being given to God's children in other parts of the country, so was not surprised to hear our girls praying in new tongues. I did not go very near these girls, lest I should stumble them by taking too much notice of them, but quietly sat down and praised God.

One Sunday, as I was coming out of the church, after the morning service, I saw some girls standing near the door of a workers' room. They seemed greatly excited and wondering. I soon found out the cause. A girl was praying aloud, and praising God in the English language. She did not know the language. Some of us gathered around her in the room, and joined her mentally in prayer. She was unconscious of what was going on, and was speaking to the Lord Jesus fluently in English. Before, I had heard her and some other girls uttering only a few syllables. Some repeated certain words over and over again. Some spoke one or more sentences, and some were simply groaning as if under a great agony of heart and mind, and carrying a great burden for souls.

"For with stammering lips and another tongue will He speak to this people."

The gift of prophecy was also given to many of the praying girls, so that they could give God's message in very clear language, taught by the Holy Spirit. The believers and unbelievers were moved alike by these messages, and a deep spiritual work began in our midst.

They who have received the gift of tongues are not using them for delivering messages from the Scriptures, except those who have received the gift of interpretation. They pray and praise God, and sometimes sing hymns in unknown tongues.
—Mukti Prayer Bell

Multitudes in India and China are starving on account of the failure of crops. Any who want to help the famine sufferers can do so by sending money to the "Apostolic Faith," and it will be sent direct to the missionaries in those countries to feed and care for the starving people, especially the orphans.

Thirteen

FIRES ARE BEING KINDLED BY THE HOLY GHOST THROUGHOUT THE WORLD, MAY 1908

THE APOSTOLIC FAITH

"Earnestly contend for the faith which was once delivered unto the saints."—Jude 3

Vol. 11, No. 13, Los Angeles, Cal., May, 1908, Subscription Free

IRELAND

Both Belfast and Bangor have been visited with Pentecost.

ENGLAND

In the past year, news comes that probably 500 people have received the Pentecost in England.

CHINA

We hear from South China that about 100 have received the baptism of the Holy Ghost and they now have a paper in the Chinese called "Pentecostal Truths," which is being scattered in China and Japan. It is a blessed paper and one can feel the power in it even though unable to read it.

WEST AFRICA

Brother E. McCauley from Long Beach, California, opened a mission in Monrovia, Liberia. God has been blessing the work. Other missionaries are helping. Sister Harmon writes: "It is marvelous at times to see the manifestations of the Spirit and to feel the power. They shake like a person with a hard chill; they are in such earnestness when they pray and God does so bless them, until you can hear them a block away."

JERUSALEM

One native minister of Beyroute, Syria, came to Jerusalem to spend the winter. God has baptized him with the Holy Ghost and he speaks with tongues. Praise God! God started this movement in A. D. 33 in this dear old city, and the "latter rain" is falling in 1908. Glory to God! Miss Elizabeth Brown of the Christian and Missionary Alliance, received her baptism more than two weeks ago. She had the real old-fashioned manifestations like many had at Azusa Street. The secret of the matter was she was so given up to God. Praise His name! She came to my room and requested me to lay hands on her for her baptism. She felt waves of fire passing through her head and face and then began to speak in tongues. She sings the heavenly chant. It is precious to hear her. —Lucy M. Leatherman, Jerusalem, Palestine, care of American Consulate

SWEDEN

The Holy Ghost is falling on the humble in Gottenberg. In one prayer meeting, they saw fire, and four persons were filled with the Holy Ghost and spoke with tongues. They praised God until 5 o'clock in the morning. In a few days, more than twelve persons were baptized with the Holy Ghost and speaking in tongues.

Eight little children have been filled with the Spirit, speaking in tongues. Some of them stand on a chair testifying for Christ.

Many sick have been healed, sinners saved and backsliders coming to the Lord. One day in February, twenty-three were baptized in water in the name of Jesus Christ. Nearly all of them had their Pentecostal experience. Many are seeking the power of God day and night.

One night the Lord sent a fisherman from an island near the city, using this dear brother in the healing of four sick people and two sisters got their baptism of the Holy Ghost at the same time.

Many sinners have come to God in different parts of Sweden. There are Pentecostal companies here and there where the Lord is taking out a people for His name. A number of workers who received their baptism in Los Angeles are there being used of God. —Brother Andrew G. Johnson, Backevick, 3 Hisingstad, Sweden

INDIA

In Panditta Ramabai's School at Mukti, Kedagon, India, God is working in power among the girls again. God is pouring out upon them such a spirit of prayer again. It is like the mighty roaring of the sea when they begin. The workers are looking for a great outpouring of His Spirit again upon Mukti. He has also been blessedly working among the Christian and Missionary Alliance people in Bombay.

Brother Max Wood Moorhead of Bombay, India, writes: "God is working mightily through the Bombay Presidency and there are witnesses now at Bombay, Khamgaon, Okola, Amraoki, Dholka, Dharangaon, Rhesqaon, Nasrapur, Pandharpur and Dhond. Praise God! Many natives are entering in, and how blessedly God uses these ignorant, lowly Indians as channels of blessing to their own people. A native boy of 19 was filled with the Holy Ghost in January and has been wonderfully healed of consumption and instrumental in winning souls to Jesus, his heathen mother and a heathen lad, an old friend. He has also been a messenger of power to missionaries from the homeland. At Dolka, a station of the Christian and Missionary Alliance, where five missionaries have received Pentecost, six orphan lads are magnifying God in new tongues."

PENTECOSTAL OUTPOURING IN SCOTLAND

FROM "CONFIDENCE," A FREE PENTECOSTAL PAPER, TO BE OBTAINED FROM THE EDITORS, 11 PARK LEA ROAD, SUNDERLAND, ENGLAND

Pentecost has fallen in Scotland at Edinburgh, Glasgow, Dumnfermline, Sterling, Clydebank, Falkirk, Tarbert, Toll Cross, Banton by Kilsyth, Kirkintillock, Coatbridge and other places.

Some incidents are reported from Kilsyth, a small Scottish town twelve miles from Glasgow, and other points.

A fireman at the colliery, as he was leaning on his shovel at work, began to speak in tongues.

A pitman at Motherwell broke out in the face of the coal—that is, while filling his wagon or tub. He was singing, "How I love that sweet story of old."

He said he felt something go down and then come up. Then for two hours he sat on his coal pile speaking in tongues as the Holy Spirit gave him utterance. The men nearby working soon heard him, and one cried: "There's Jock through in tongues and me no saved yet."

A number have been converted just through hearing others speak in tongues. It was so with young H. He loved cycle-racing, etc., and kept away from the meetings; but when he heard his sister "speaking mysteries" praising God in an unknown tongue, he was broken down. In the Mission Hall, from 3 one afternoon till 2 the next morning, he dealt with God and was saved, sanctified, and baptized with the Holy Ghost with the Scriptural evidences.

In a village in this part of Scotland, the little chapel got on fire and about twenty received their Pentecost with signs following and thirteen have been soundly converted. They were holding a "fellowship meeting" for those who had been fully anointed. Outsiders hearing the vehement cries of praise and the speaking in tongues, gathered around. A sympathetic policeman kept the door (his wife and daughter, who had received the blessing were inside). At last he cried, "Lads, I can stand it no longer, here goes." And he flung open the door, and putting down his helmet, was soon pleading with God for the full baptism of the Holy Ghost. And he received it then and there and came through speaking in tongues.

It is touching to see the boys at Kilsyth (quite a number have got their Pentecost) all with their Bibles in the meeting, and little girls, too, speaking in tongues and giving out solemn messages.

In other places children have had to suffer. We have heard of one whose father in the drink, kicked his little girl because she went to the meetings, and she looking up at him, and through her tears, said, "Glory to Jesus!"

An engine driver at Kilsyth was making his way to the house, and his legs gave way. The power of God fell on him, and they supported him to Brother Murdoch's kitchen where many have received the baptism, and he was soon "through," singing as the Spirit gave him utterance, and has been singing ever since.

Many have already traveled to Kilsyth from the east and west, the north and south. Some critical investigators arrived one day by train. They agreed to test this thing by putting questions to the first Kilsyth man they met. It was the porter who opened the carriage door.

"Any meetings being held here?"

"Aye, sir, there are."

"Have you been to any of them?"

"Yes, I've been."

"Is it true that some folks are speaking in tongues?"

"It's true enough."

"Do you know anyone?"

"Yes, I'm one myself."

Scottish people know their Bibles. They are no fools, not carried away easily. But they know that God has appeared in their midst, and they praise Him and exalt the ever-precious Blood by which victory is insured.

PENTECOST IN AUSTRALIA

THE LORD HAS VISITED AUSTRALIA IN GREAT POWER AND SOULS HAVE BEEN BAPTIZED WITH THE HOLY GHOST AND SIGNS FOLLOWING.

In a cottage meeting, in February, 1907, in Melbourne, a young brother received the baptism of the Holy Ghost and began to speak in tongues. Some fell under the power of God, and a great awe came over the meeting. The brother spoke and sang, giving messages in the unknown tongue and also interpreting.

A few Christians stopped at the house on the way to church one Saturday night, but said they would have a little time of prayer first. The Lord came down in such power that they could not go, and some spoke in tongues and sang heavenly music.

A sister was washing up the breakfast things, when the Lord called her to prayer, she immediately obeyed Him, and the Spirit soon led her off in praise to Him in an unknown tongue. She says, "I was simply lost in His love."

A few were waiting upon God one Friday night when the Holy Spirit fell upon a lad of 19. He sang beautifully for over an hour about Jesus' coming. Next morning while at work, he sang praises to God in an unknown tongue.

These great blessings have come upon the lowly and humble. Many have seen visions of Jesus and of heavenly fire, and the interpretations speak of the soon coming of Jesus.

A burglar came to the altar at Azusa Mission, threw his skeleton keys under the bench (he had been plotting to rob a house). He got gloriously saved, soon he was sanctified. He was baptized down at the ocean and shouted and jumped in the water and out of the water, he was so filled with the power of God. That afternoon he was baptized with the Holy Ghost and spake in tongues. He praises God and weeps as he tells of His wonderful love and mercy.

A sister finding there were some things hindering from getting her baptism, shut herself in her room and prayed practically all day and all night. She prayed through and got all her idols out of her heart and the power fell on her "like hail," she says. She talked in tongues for a long time, though she said when she came to the mission that she did not want tongues. But God baptized her like all the rest.

A brother came from China to Los Angeles and received the baptism of the Holy Ghost and went on his way to England, and writes that it was the most wonderful experience of his life and he is rejoicing in the fullness of the Spirit.

The leading man among the colored Freemasons in Indianapolis and who was also cartoonist for two newspapers, was sanctified and baptized with the Holy Ghost speaking in divers new tongues. He resigned and had prayer with his members in the lodge room, and they were much touched. Some of his brethren have since received their Pentecost also.

What hath God wrought? In two precious years since the Lord poured out the Pentecost in Los Angeles in a little cottage on Bonnie Brae Street, He has spread it around the world. Hallelujah. Many are rejoicing with joy unspeakable for the great blessings that

God is pouring out in this latter rain. Many saved, sanctified, healed of disease and baptized with the Holy Ghost and fire. Many happy families filled with the Spirit and working for Jesus. Soon after the Pentecost fell, the saints rented the lower room in the old building on Azusa Street, which has been much blest of God. To Him be all the glory and praise. When the place was about to be sold so that the Mission would have to move, the saints agreed to purchase it with three years' time to pay the $15,000, expecting the Lord to send the money all in before that time, and He has done it and answered our prayers in a wonderful way. We humbly thank God. We love to think of the blessed old "Manger Home" where so many of us have received the baptism of the Holy Ghost. Many saints love the spot, and will rejoice that God has given it to us.

Christ's character is our pattern and His word is our discipline. We want to be just like Jesus in His suffering, His passion, His death. He is our ideal. Glory to God!

Chinese Pentecostal Paper— The Lord laid it on my heart to get out a paper in the Chinese language. I put it before my Chinese brethren and they prayed over it and God put it at once on their hearts, and they began to translate pieces into Chinese. God has given us a Chinese brother who has received the baptism of the Holy Ghost and is a good printer. The paper is already being scattered among the millions in China. Offerings to help the dear Chinese brethren, who are poor in this world's goods, get out their paper and circulate this Gospel, may be sent to Brother Mok Lai Chi, 5 Laddes St., Hong Kong, China.—Bro. McIntosh

-----

Word comes that Bishop Horner of the Holiness movement of Canada has been baptized with the Holy Ghost as on the day of Pentecost. He had been claiming his baptism for twenty years and he says this is the greatest baptism he ever had.

Two Pentecostal papers in the Norwegian language are being published, the "Sandhedans Tolk," published by Brother H. Langeland, Pausbo, Wash., and "Byposten," by Brother T. B. Barratt, Christiania, Norway.

The Lord has baptized a number in the little faith cottage back of the Mission. He has used our dear Sister Farrow whom He sent from Texas at the beginning of the outpouring of the Spirit in Los Angeles. In her room in the cottage, quite a number have received a greater filling of the Spirit and some have been healed and baptized with the Spirit since she returned from Africa.

Character and Work of the Holy Ghost. His character is love. If you find people that get a harsh spirit, and even talk in tongues in a harsh spirit, it is not the Holy Ghost talking. His utterances are in power and glory and with blessing and sweetness. The character of the Holy Ghost is precisely like Jesus the Word of truth, for the Holy Ghost is "the Spirit of Truth." He speaks always of the Word and makes everything like the Word. Jesus was the Son of God, the suffering Christ; and the Holy Ghost comes into the world to reveal this suffering Christ to us. He is a meek and humble Spirit—not a harsh Spirit. He is a Spirit of glory. When He comes into a believer, He comes to tell them all about Jesus' salvation. He reveals Christ. He paints Him as the wonderful Son of God, the brightest gem the Father had in heaven, our only hope of salvation and reconciliation with the Father. How sweet it is to have the Holy Ghost come to you and show you Jesus through the Word, and never gets outside of the Word.

Every man born of the Spirit is born of Jesus Christ. The new birth puts you into the church and sin puts you out.

No wonder people get the missionary spirit as soon as they get the baptism because they become partners with the Holy Spirit.

In the baptism of the Spirit, you are under the power of the Spirit, and do not have to judge by what your eyes see and your ears hear but what the Spirit reveals.

NOTES

1. Vinson Synan, ed., *The Century of the Holy Spirit* (Nashville: Thomas Nelson, 2001), 371.

2. *The Dallas Morning News*, Saturday, December 4, 1999, 4 G.

3. *The Dallas Morning News*, Saturday, December 4, 1999, 4 G.

4. John G. Lake, *Spiritual Hunger/The God-Men* (Dallas: Christ for the Nations, 1980), 13.

5. "When the Spirit Fell in Los Angeles: An Eye-Witness Account," *Pentecostal Evangel* (April 6, 1946): 6–7.

6. *The Apostolic Faith*, May 1907, compiled by Fred T. Corum, *Like As of Fire* (Wilmington, MA: Corum, Fall 1988), 3.

7. "When the Spirit Fell in Los Angeles: An Eye-Witness Account," 7.

8. Frank Bartleman, *Azusa Street*, ed. Vinson Synan. (Plainfield: Logos, 1980), 60.

9. Lake, *Spiritual Hunger/The God-Men*, 14.

10. Bartleman, *Azusa Street*, 59–60.

11. Bartleman, *Azusa Street*, 54.

12. Vinson Synan, *The Holiness-Pentecostal Movement in the United States* (Grand Rapids: Eerdmans, 1971), 109.

13. Ernest S. Williams, "Memories of Azusa Street Mission," Pentecostal Vertical File, Holy Spirit Research Center Oral Roberts University, 1.

14. Williams, "Memories of the Azusa Street Mission," 1.

15. Synan, 109.

16. Bartleman, 54.

17. These words appear in the subtitle of Harvey Cox, *Fire From Heaven: The Rise of Pentecostal Spirituality and the Reshaping of Religion in the Twenty-first Century* (Reading, MA; New York: Addison-Wesley, 1995).

INDEX